E

Homemade Healthy Dog Food

Cookbook for Nutritious House Made Meals and Treats with 144 Easy Recipes

DJTS
PUBLISHING

Table of Contents

The Best Food for Your Best Friend

Welcome to the wonderful world of cooking for your furry best friend. How much do you know about what goes into your dog's diet? There are so many options on the market today that claim to offer a balanced diet, but it can be hard to sift through all of them and figure out which one is best for your pooch. Your dog is a member of your family, which means you'll want to discover a meal that tastes wonderful and contains the proper balance of nutrients for your best friend's development and health.

My husband and I are pet parents who share our time with our canine family members, just like you. We recognized the importance of these beloved companions to our everyday lives, so we go out of our way to provide them with the finest care possible. I enjoy making dishes for our dogs from local ingredients, including many meals that we all share. I love to create doggy dinners, the occasional special celebratory meal, or everyday dog treats - and it's always greatly appreciated!

This book is particularly useful for dog owners looking for healthy alternatives to commercial dog foods. Perhaps you don't want your dogs to be exposed to the preservatives and additives present in many store-bought dog treats. Perhaps you enjoy cooking and want to provide your dog with nutritious dishes cooked from in-season produce. Perhaps your dog requires a specialty diet that is expensive to obtain. There is no one-size-fits-all diet for all dogs, just as there is no one-size-fits-all diet for all people. Each dog is unique, and some will flourish on one diet while others will thrive on another. Many pet owners wish to provide their dogs with a nutritious specialist diet. This cookbook has dish examples for whatever type of diet your dog needs, from grain-free to Paleo to raw to traditional.

If in doubt, you should work with your veterinarian to discover the ideal diets for your dog's breed, energy level, and life stage. By preparing food at home, you are able to closely monitor what your dog is eating, which can be especially beneficial for puppies and senior dogs.

This cookbook is not just for dogs with special dietary needs. You may want to prepare your dog's food because you feel it is the best option for his or her overall health. Unlike cats, which are obligate carnivores and require a meat-based diet, dogs eat and enjoy a variety of foods. The canine diet naturally leans primarily toward meat, as seen by your dog's teeth, which are designed to tear rather than chew and grind. However, canines can digest and enjoy a wide variety of fruits and vegetables. Bananas, blueberries, blackberries, and other fruits will add flavor to your dog's treats and meals while also providing good nourishment. Don't overlook the vegetables, dogs enjoy fresh vegetables! I included recipes for numerous seasonal favorites, such as sweet potato and pumpkin, as well as many dishes that serve as a template for employing your dog's favorite vegetables depending on the season.

This book will expose you to a variety of nutritious cuisine that you may proudly offer to your furry friends. You'll allow them to enjoy their food and goodies while still living healthy lives.

We didn't use color printing or images in this book because I wanted to minimize the effect on the environment as much as possible. I hope you enjoy cooking from this cookbook!

The Art of Cooking for Your Dog

Many dog owners underestimate how much nutrition goes into their furry companions' food. A balanced diet is key to keeping your furry friend healthy and happy for his or her entire life; however, it isn't always easy to know what your dog's nutritional needs are. You can also use this cookbook to ensure that Fido eats well-rounded meals and treats every other day of the week!

Why make your own dog food when you can buy it ready-made? It's really straightforward: You get full control over the ingredients that went into it. You control what your dog consumes when you prepare it yourself; thus, you can tailor the meal to individual demands. Furthermore, when you cook for yourself, you may adjust the meal to your dog's requirements. This is especially beneficial for sick dogs that are unable to eat certain items owing to allergies or medication. If your dog is overweight, you can help him or her lose weight by providing the appropriate meals.

If you prepare your dog's food, there is more variety in the dish, which most dogs like. Making your own meals also implies using the appropriate balance of components to guarantee that your dog receives all of the necessary minerals.

It's vital to remember that the dishes should be prepared with fresh ingredients. Use your local butcher for meat, fresh produce and herbs from your garden, and high-quality grains - preferably organic. Of course, it goes without saying that you should always verify the freshness of your ingredients before putting them in the dish.

If your dogs are on a diet, you should attempt to prepare meals that are appetizing enough to persuade them not to "cheat" when they eating healthy foods. I'll give you a plethora of tasty options for this purpose.

In my opinion, the greatest benefit of feeding homemade dog food is that you can control the feed's quality. At the same time, you take responsibility for making sure your dogs have all of the necessities they require to maintain their health. To have this done on your own will take some effort in the beginning. But it also sets you free from the food industry since you are no longer dependent on them. Homemade food does not need a lengthy list of ingredients to be comprehended by you. Plus, you may simply omit any food that your dog can't stomach, such as grain.

There are many different types of meals that you can offer to a dog since they are omnivores. Our dogs eat potatoes with cooked chicken, carrots, some fennel, and a teaspoon of linseed oil on one day. On other days, they will receive rice with cottage cheese and boiled ground beef. Some vegetables, on the other hand, are not as popular with them. They also enjoy meals that are completely vegetarian, such as soaked oat flakes, grated apple and pear, some quark, an egg, and a teaspoon of rapeseed oil.

When it comes to preparing it, there are no restrictions! Of course, except for the foods that dogs are sensitive to.

Living a Healthy Dog Life

In this chapter you will learn all the basics your dog needs to have a healthy life. Dogs don't reliably know which food is healthy and which isn't. Dogs get fat from overeating, especially from table scraps. In hot weather a dog can easily overheat because most breeds have little or no ability to sweat. Your dog can't ask you for water, so it is up to you to look after his or her hydration needs.

Before starting to cook some good-looking recipes, it is important to know how to maintain your dog's health and what can negatively affect it. Dogs' very efficient digestive tracts can handle a surprising amount of abuse, but that doesn't mean that they should get it.

Having a healthy dog is not only about feeding him or her good food with the right number of proteins, carbs and fats. There are also several other factors that influence your dog's health and we will go into more detail about the most important ones.

Approaches to Feeding Your Dog

There are many different approaches to nutrition that revolve around the same general principal - a well-balanced meal. No matter which nutritional approach you prefer, it is important to know which components are vital to your dog's well-being.

Fresh homemade food

A dog's diet must include all of the required nutrients, vitamins and minerals in order for it to be healthy. To prevent deficiency symptoms, the feed's composition must be varied and balanced. All of the needs can be easily provided by fresh homemade food. On top of that, fresh food tastes better than commercial food. In this book I will provide you with a great variety of recipes that are made from only fresh ingredients.

Ready-made food

Ready-made food provides dogs with nutrients, but it is full of additives that neither you nor your dog needs. There are many well-known brands in the market, but they vary greatly in their quality. There are many different types of ready-made dog food, but it is advisable to stay away from them under normal circumstances. Some of the ingredients in ready-made dog food are not very good for a dog's health and may cause digestive problems.

Kibble

Kibble is a staple in many households, but it isn't very healthy since it has a lot of carbohydrates. People who have a problem with their dog's weight should stay away from this dry food since it is very rich in carbs and many dogs will simply overeat. There is also a risk that your dog will suffer from obesity and related problems such as diabetes and arthritis. Dog food manufacturers say that dogs need a high level of carbohydrates in their diet, but they are just making money. Carbohydrates may be used as an effective filler.

Dog treats

Some dog treats may appear healthy and some unhealthy, but it is very easy to overfeed and that is never good. It isn't healthy to feed your dog treats on a regular basis. A treat has to be implemented into the daily amount of food. In this book, you will find a lot of ideas and recipes for delicious and healthy treats.

Raw diet

This term means that you feed your dog raw meat, bones, and fresh fruits and vegetables. This type of diet is used a lot in the US, but it is very controversial. Many veterinarians are against the idea of feeding raw meat to dogs since it may have harmful bacteria or parasites that can be transferred to your dog. You can find some recipes for raw food in this book.

Paleo Diet

The paleo diet is rich in proteins and very low on carbs. This type of diet has only recently become popular, but it works great for dogs. If you're looking for recipes that are suited for a paleo diet, you will find some in this book.

Vegetarian diet

A solely vegetarian diet for dogs is not very healthy for your dog and can result in long-term nutritional deficiencies. Of course, this is only a problem if you do it exclusively. In this book, you'll find numerous vegetarian dishes, but make sure to include some meat meals in your dog's diet as well.

Fresh drinking water in clean containers must be accessible to your dog at all times, regardless of the type of food you offer.

No matter what you feed your dog, make sure you do it responsibly and measure the amounts. There are many types of food and treats that you can prepare for your dog at home and I will tell you more about them in the following chapters.

The Trouble of Finding the Right Diet for Your Dog

The discussion about the best food and feeding method for four-legged friends has become a divisive issue for many dog owners, and it is frequently disputed with very strong opinions. In most cases, the focus is on "how" (raw, cooked, or ready) and leads to a war of attrition over the best, most natural (or rather least processed) food for dogs. There's food for Golden Retrievers, small dogs, city dogs or even indoor mini dogs. Is raw feeding the greatest, or should you offer your dog paleo meals? What about leftovers?

What you should focus on is the "what," which refers to the ideal balance of nutrients and minerals. Aside from the obvious health benefits, the components of dog food have a big impact on the animal's behavior. The form in which you feed the ingredients is rather secondary for most dogs. There is a big difference between dogs, but most of the time the problem isn't the dog – it's us humans.

Healthy Lifestyle for Your Dog

What else should you know about your dog's health? On top of a balanced diet, your dogs should receive regular checkups at the veterinarian's office and receive adequate body care. With these, you can rest assured that your dog will most likely enjoy a long and happy dog life.

Care

Regular body care is not only for hygiene's sake, but it also aids in the development of a dog-human relationship. It's a component of canine education, in which the dog is informed that you are the leader of the pack. Your dog must accept care and obey your instructions. The level of care required varies by breed. Breed-specific care instructions should be obtained from the breeder or a competent organization.

Hair care

Hair care varies significantly depending on your dog's coat type (short, rough, long, stick hair, etc.). Dogs should be brushed or combed on a regular basis, and their fur might also need to be trimmed depending on the breed. Bathe your dog with a soap that is designed to moisturize.

Eye care

The eyes of your dog should be cleaned on a regular basis if the eye secretion accumulates in the corner of the eye and is not removed by your dog. This will avoid inflammation and eye infection. When cleaning the eyes, use a damp cloth and wipe from the nose to the outer corner of the eye.

Ear care

Once or twice a week, your dog's ears should be inspected. Because the external ear canal is difficult to access, it is not advised to clean it oneself. Using cotton swabs (Q-tips or similar) in particular runs the danger of injuring your dog and introducing dirt or other foreign objects into the ear canal. If required, the veterinarian should be consulted.

Denture care

The teeth should be cleaned using buffalo skin bones, hard dog biscuits, and other things of that sort. The dog should chew on them and then be given its regular food to swallow after, which will carry the pieces of bone down to the stomach. Alternatively, you can use regular bones or canine toothpaste, which is designed to clean the teeth and also reduce bad breath. If plaque or inflammation are severe, the veterinarian should be consulted.

Claw care

Dog claws are constantly growing. They should be cut regularly, so it is advised to use claw trimmers. They're important for your dog's balance. If they are too long, it can cause pain and even limping. If your dog is getting enough exercise, the claws will wear down naturally.

Regular checkups

For your dog to be healthy, it's important that you regularly take him or her for checkups with the veterinarian. These visits are also a good opportunity for you to ask any questions you might have. Because your dog can't tell you when he or she is in pain, it's up to you to pay attention. The veterinarian will also check if your dog is in good health and inform you of the necessary vaccinations before they are due.

Your dog needs exercise too

It's not just food that makes your dog healthy, exercising is equally important. Just like us, dogs require exercise to keep their muscles in shape and maintain a healthy weight. If you own more than one dog, it's important to adjust the amount of exercise to each dog's individual needs. If your dog is getting enough exercise, you should be able to feel the ribs when you rub his or her side. However, a dog should never be bony or have a protruding backbone either.

The dire consequences of an unhealthy lifestyle

A sedentary lifestyle combined with an unhealthy diet often results in obesity. Obese dogs can develop serious health problems such as arthritis, heart disease, and other joint diseases. If your dog constantly begs at the table or constantly thinks about food, he or she is probably overweight.

Improve Your Dog's Well-being for a Long Life

As pet parents, we are committed to making sure that our four-legged companion have a happy, healthy and long existence. Here are some pointers for creating a happy, healthy dog existence for your pet.

Lots of exercise

Exercising with your pet is not only good for their health, but it also boosts their happiness hormones, builds up their immune system, improves circulation and trains the muscles.

Every dog requires exercise. The amount and frequency depend on the dog's age and breed. Young dogs and small dogs (shoulder height up to 35 cm) should have the opportunity to run for between 15 and 30 minutes several times a day. It's essential to alternate between intense phases that test the animal and quieter phases for rest. It is enough for large adult dogs to exercise twice a day for one hour at a slow pace and 15 minutes of fast play.

Dogs that have been bred for hunting, greyhounds, or huskies, require a lot of exercise. In order to exercise, these dogs require an additional hour of play every day or a compensatory dog activity in addition to their regular runs.

If you have short-nosed dogs, such as bulldogs or pugs, you should avoid overdoing it with the activities. The amount of walking steps should be decreased, and other forms of physical activity, such as search games, should be performed.

In general, keep an eye on variety. Do not always do the same laps, but switch to an activity that your dog loves, such as searching or playing. Take a bike ride, go on a leashed walk in the woods, or go to the beach and play ball. As a result, you can be confident that your dog's desire to walk will be satisfied and the happy hormones will surge.

Protect skin and fur

The skin is not only your best friend's largest organ, but it also serves as an important protective covering and sign of how well he or she is. If the fur appears flaky or dull, it is an indication that your dog is unwell, malnourished, stressed, or allergic. Skin diseases can also be caused by food allergies, hormonal problems and autoimmune diseases in which the dog's own antibodies attack the skin.

Fungal infections are more common in young animals or those with a weakened immune system. The most common location for these to grow is on the face or ears. Circular bald patches are indicators of a fungal infection, as well. Because the fungus can be transferred to humans, you should also be cautious.

Avoid poisonous substances

There are several hazardous items in our kitchens and medicine cabinets that are harmful to dogs. We'll delve into greater depth later on. Dogs may be poisoned by food or other items that appear to be tasty or helpful to humans.

A common example is chocolate. Because dogs are unable to break down theobromine, chocolate and other cocoa products can be deadly to them. Vomiting, diarrhea, shakes, and cardiac failure are typical symptoms of poisoning that appear two to twelve hours after ingestion. Coffee, energy drinks, and cola can all lead to the same symptoms and effects.

Dogs should avoid onion, garlic, and chives since they are poisonous to them. Even after ingesting only modest amounts (5-10 g per kg of body weight), sulfur compounds in the food cause hemolysis (destruction of the red blood cells). Vomiting and diarrhea, followed by a loss of appetite, weakness, increased breathing and cardiac rate, pale mucous membranes and urine that is red or brown in color can all be symptoms and signs of poisoning.

Because it does not cause tooth decay, birch sugar xylitol is gaining in popularity among individuals seeking for a healthy sugar substitute. However, it can result in a significant insulin release in dogs, which can lead to a severe blood sugar drop. Birch sugar is also toxic to dogs' livers, and it has the potential to induce liver failure.

Hygiene

You should also be concerned about cleanliness when having a dog. If you make sure that your four-legged companion is fragrant and pure, you will not only do your nose a favor, but you will also prevent many problems such as matted hair, skin irritations, infections and parasite infestation.

You should be diligent about their hair, particularly when it comes to long-haired dogs. In the summer, especially when it's hot, extra fur is agony for the animal.

Not only should the dog be kept clean, but so should its surroundings. Bacteria love to crawl about in dirty food bowls and their surrounds, as well as sleeping places and litter boxes. You should make sure that these locations are cleaned on a regular basis and thoroughly. You should also clean and disinfect other objects with which your pet has frequent contact on a regular basis.

Protect your dog from heat

Summer is a time for us to enjoy, but when the thermometer rises, our dogs easily become overheated. In extreme circumstances, the heat is a burden on the animal's circulation and may even be deadly.

During the summer months, it's especially critical for dogs to have enough drinking water on hand. Make sure the drinking water bowl is always completely filled. If you're out and about with your dog, bring a water bottle with you and offer water to drink.

Food is more difficult to digest when it is extremely hot. It's preferable to prepare small portions at this stage and serve them early in the morning or late at night, when it's cooler. Wet food spoils quickly in the summer months, therefore it should not be kept for too long. Flies lay their eggs in it and it spoils rapidly.

When the dog's temperature begins to rise, he or she might begin panting and becoming unresponsive. If your dog begins to stagger and has a glassy stare, vomits, and the tongue gets dark, it is a sign of a heat stroke. Put your dog in the shade and wet down its legs first, then its entire body with cold towels. Give your dog lukewarm water to drink and go to the nearest veterinarian as soon as possible.

Sleep and rest

A good night's sleep for your dog is essential for his or her physical and emotional well-being. Your dog needs a lot of rest and sleep to regenerate after a day of running around. A good night's sleep not only rejuvenates the dog, but also has a positive effect on his or her behavior.

As a result, you should ensure that your dog has a peaceful corner in which it may relax and sleep undisturbed. We want to eliminate any sound that might cause distractions, such as traffic noise or the continual opening and closing of doors. Your dog may become annoyed by the same factors that irritate you and make you irritable: sleeplessness, loud noises, and so on.

The amount of rest and relaxation that dogs require is frequently underestimated, with adult canines needing between 12 and 14 hours of sleep. This requirement is increased by a few more hours per day for young, sick, and old dogs. Naps, sunbathing or resting on the sofa with many cuddles are all included in the allotted times.

Examine your dog's current physical condition

If you discover that your dog has a few extra pounds on him, you're probably not too concerned. However, when it comes to health, size matters!

The body condition score is a score that assesses how much fat your dog has on his or her body. It's easy to do at home, and it can detect issues in overweight dogs before the scales reveal a significant change. Furthermore, because the scale is suitable for nearly every dog breed, you may easily use it between vet appointments.

It's part of being a dog owner to keep an eye on your dog's body score and strive to keep a 'perfect' four or five throughout his or her life. This will also assist to minimize the health concerns associated with having a large dog. If your dog consumes more calories than they require, these extra calories may be stored as fat and cause canine obesity.

Your puppy's chubby physique may appear to be adorable if it is still a youngster. However, keep an eye on those additional rolls of puppy fat, as they might indicate an overly fat adult dog in the future. It might be difficult for owners to tell the fluff from the fat in their puppy's first 12-18 months of life. Obese puppies are highly sensitive to the impacts of extra body fat. Obese pups are more likely to develop orthopedic problems as they mature and affect the structure of their bones and cartilage in their joints. Puppies with orthopedic issues may have restricted mobility and arthritis for the rest of their lives. Make sure you're counting the correct number of calories for your pup, and don't forget to include the treats.

Love

Last but not least, express your affection for your dog every day. Your dog is your friend and wants to feel like one. They want to be around you, even if you are busy. They want to be your best friend and your buddy, so don't let them down! If you keep your dog's needs in mind, a happy and healthy life together will be easy to maintain. With a real heart, your dog will return love and gratitude at every opportunity.

03

Nutrients and Ingredients

The phrase "complete and balanced" may be found on the label of most commercial dog foods. This is however not the same as being healthy.

In order to meet these standards, a dog food manufacturer may include several vitamins and minerals in their recipe without providing any real benefit. Look for more than just numbers of synthetic nutrients as proof that your pet's needs are being met - even if they appear on the label.

In a homemade dog food diet, you know exactly what your dog is eating. This is why it's so important to have a thorough knowledge about the nutrients that are suitable for your type of dog. You are also able to create meals with higher amounts of certain nutrients if they are beneficial to your pet.

It's critical that dogs eat a well-balanced diet, but it doesn't mean every meal has to be perfectly balanced. It's about having the right food combinations throughout the week, giving your dog all of their required nutrients. Your dog's diet can be varied from meal to meal, balancing out throughout the course of the week's breakfasts and dinners.

In this chapter you will learn how to prepare your dog meals. You will learn how to feed him, how much food your dog needs and when you should provide your dog more or less food.

Guide to Nutrients

To be able to feed your dog the best meals, learn about nutrition and vitamins. Healthy food means nothing unless it contains all of the required substances that contribute to health maintenance and disease prevention.

Protein

Protein is an essential part of a dog's diet, providing the amino acids that are vital for growth. In regards to food quality, protein from animal sources is more beneficial than vegetable sources. Protein from meat and eggs have a perfect profile of amino acids, while vegetable proteins lack certain ones. Vegetables can still provide substantial amounts of protein for your dog, but you'll need to mix it with other types of protein.

Every cell in the body contains protein, making it an essential component of meals. Your dog and you need it to retain your body's structure. Protein is also required in larger amounts as a result of physical activity and the need for growing pups. The more excellent the protein, the less of it a dog will require. The greater the amount of exercise a dog gets, the higher his or her protein requirement. Also, in unusual situations, such as illness or recuperation, our dog's protein demand is increased. Pregnancy and nursing are the most significant factors that influence a dog's protein requirement.

Fat

Fat is an important part of your dog's diet. The best fat comes from animal sources, because their bodies are able to process it more easily than plant-based fats. It is true that fat has 9 calories per gram, but your dog needs it for energy and to absorb vitamins such as A, D, and E.

Carbohydrates

Carbohydrates are the primary source of energy for your dog. Carbohydrates provide glucose to cells and can be converted into glycogen, which is stored in the muscles and liver. Dogs don't have to eat carbohydrates, but they will get more energy from them compared to other sources of energy.

Vegetables are able to provide carbohydrates. Dogs can turn veggies into glucose for energy, but it takes more effort than getting the same amount of energy from a meat-based diet.

If your dog is overweight, carbohydrates should be limited. It's a very easy way to help control your dog's weight.

Magnesium

Magnesium is supposed to have stress-reducing properties. It can result in an enhanced cortisol release, meaning it affects the production of stress hormones if the mineral is adequately supplied to the body. Magnesium has calming and soothing effects on the body by dampening nerve transmission.

Stress causes an increase in the demand for magnesium by increasing consumption of the mineral in cells, as well as increased excretion. In the case of a dog that is under continual strain, magnesium should be supplied.

Calcium

Calcium is an essential part of your dog's diet. Calcium plays a vital role in the development and maintenance of bones and teeth. Having calcium-rich food available to dogs is critical because they can't produce or absorb it on their own without proper amounts.

A dog's diet needs to be supplemented with calcium if he or she is neutered, pregnant, lactating, ill or growing. If your dog is deficient in calcium, it can lead to a malfunction of their urinary system and severe health problems later on.

Calcium has some indirect affects too - for example, it can have an effect on your dog's temperament.

You'll find a method for producing your own eggshell calcium in this book, which many pet owners prefer to bone meal because bones can store calcium. Since eggshells are composed of calcium carbonate, they contain great amounts of the mineral.

Other important vitamins and minerals

Nutritional supplements are frequently added to commercial dog food recipes, in part because they are used to compensate for nutrients lost during the processing and preparation of the meals. Commercial dog food is frequently manufactured using a high-heat extrusion process, which can damage the natural nutrients. Because of this, dog food must include artificial additives to match the nutritional requirements of dogs.

Making your dog's meals from scratch will be a healthier alternative to commercial dog food because you're providing natural compounds like vitamins, minerals, protein, fiber, and fatty acids.

"If it meets my nutritional needs, it must also meet the nutritional demands of my dog." Although this may appear to make sense, it is faulty because the digestive systems of dogs and humans are not comparable. Make sure that your dog's diet includes all the necessary ingredients.

The following is a list of vitamins and minerals, which are the building blocks of your dog's diet.

- Vitamin A, which is abundant in liver and fish oil, fortifies the immune system and promotes skin, eye, and hair health.
- Vitamin B is important for the nervous system. It's also required for a dog's coat, skin, growth, and vision.
- Vitamin C has been shown to reduce inflammation, boost the immune system, and promote the growth of healthy cells. Vitamin C is found in many plant oils.
- Vitamin D: Liver is high in vitamin D, which helps to strengthen bones and teeth.
- Vitamin E, which is abundant in vegetable oils, helps to strengthen the immune system and encourage the formation of healthy cells.
- Vitamin K helps with blood clotting.
- Phosphorus is a mineral that aids in the maintenance of strong bones and teeth, as well as healthy cells and muscles. The ideal calcium-to-phosphorus ratio is crucial. This mineral can be found in meats, dairy products, and eggs.
- Sodium is important for the health of your dog's muscles and helps to maintain fluid balance.
- Copper is essential for healthy bones and preventing anemia.
- Iron is a mineral that helps to promote healthy blood and protect against fatigue and anemia.
- Zinc is essential for growth and healthy skin and coat.
- Essential fatty acids support a healthy diet and include omega-3 and omega-6 fatty acids.

- Omega-6 is necessary for your dog's coat to remain healthy and glossy, enabling it to have beautiful, luxurious fur. A little bit of sunflower or safflower oil (approximately 1 tsp for a tiny dog or 1 tbsp for a large dog) may support your dog's diet.

- Omega-3 fatty acids, which may be derived from flaxseed oil or fish oil (particularly sardines), are beneficial for your dog's skin.

Feed This: Ingredients That are Good for Your Dog

There are numerous types of ingredients you can feed your dog. A little bit of everything is needed for a healthy diet, so remember that variety is important for your canine companion.

I compiled a list of the most important dog diet components allowing you to make your own decisions. Although many dogs have special nutritional needs and allergies, the following are the most important components for optimal health and nutrition.

Meat

Meat is high in protein, which your pet needs to burn energy. It is the most important entry on this list because your dog can't live a healthy live without it. There are a ton of different animal sources that you can substitute in a recipe, but the most common types include chicken, turkey, beef or fish. Note that some dogs have allergies or conditions to specific sources of meat so try to mix it up as much as possible.

Vegetables

Vegetables are the easiest to substitute in recipes, but you can always add something fresh if you please. Vegetables in your dog's diet may be quite beneficial, as they provide a variety of vitamins and minerals. Just like with humans, some veggies are better than others and certain dogs will react poorly to others. Common veggies that you can use include peas, carrots, broccoli, or spinach. Sweet potatoes are high in potassium, vitamin B, and beta-carotene, as well as antioxidants that help to prevent cancer.

Fruits

Dogs can thrive on fruits because they are high in nutrients and fiber to aid digestion. Fruits can also be used to add flavor for picky eaters or dogs with digestion problems. Some fruits are toxic to dogs, but there are many types of berries that are safe. Berries can also be used to make homemade dog treats. Blueberries and apples are high in fiber, vitamin C, and antioxidants. Cranberries may aid in the treatment of urinary tract infections and dental health.

Fatty foods

Fatty foods are a great way to add flavor to your dog's food without adding too many calories. Your kitchen might already contain a variety of fats, but keep in mind that the wrong form of fat is bad for dogs. All of us have heard about the dangers of fats, but they are actually required for cell function and digestion. High-quality fats, such as Omega-3 and Omega-6 fatty acids, fish oils, canola oil, chicken fat, and olive oil, should be preferred.

Organ meat

Organ meats, like lean, muscle-based protein, are an essential component in dog meals. Organ meats are an excellent source of nourishment for dogs when compared to their own diet. Organ meat is also high in protein and provides a ton of essential vitamins and minerals for your dog. When wolves consume organ meats, they are able to obtain all of the nutrients and vitamins that they require. Organ meats, such as the kidneys, heart, liver, and poultry gizzard, are highly recommended.

Vitamins

They are important for all aspects of the body's metabolism, digestive process, and immunological system, as well as nerve and blood cell health. B-vitamins, such as biotin, pyridoxine, riboflavin, thiamin, and beta-carotene, should be at focused on. Vitamin A is critical for your dog's skin and coat. Vitamin E benefits your dog's immune system.

Minerals and nutrients

Zinc, iron, potassium, calcium, and manganese are all essential minerals for a dog's health. L Carnitine is a vitamin that aids in the cellular generation of energy and works as a transport for fatty acids. DL- Methionine, one of the 10-plus essential amino acids required by dogs is also crucial.

Superfoods

Although there are many types of superfoods for dogs, they do deserve special attention. Superfoods are nutritional superheroes for dogs. Chia seeds, blueberries, pumpkin, kale, and quinoa are among the finest superfoods for dogs.

Water

In order to maintain a healthy weight, proper exercise, organ function and digestion, as well as an ample supply of vitamins and minerals, water is essential. Your dog's water should be clean, fresh, and appealing to drink. It should be un-chlorinated and filtered to remove impurities. Make sure your dog has access to fresh, clean water at all times.

Carbohydrates

Most dogs, like humans, must acquire a taste for vegetables and fruits first. A daily consumption of vegetables and fruit is essential for your dog's optimum health. When you start feeding your dog a diet rich in vegetables and fruits, they will quickly realize how delicious vegetables can be.

Grains and carbohydrates are one of the components in dog food that some people despise, but they aren't nearly as bad as many people believe. In fact, wild dogs and wolves regularly consume their prey's stomach content first, which often include grains and plant materials. Carbohydrates give your dog a lot of energy, and high-quality grains might help with digestion. Make sure you do not overdo it with carbohydrates and grains because it can lead to weight gain.

Do Not Feed This: Unhealthy and Toxic Ingredients

Certain meals should not be given to dogs since they might be harmful or poisonous to them. Do you feed your dog food that has been cooked for humans? It is critical to correct this behavior. Unfortunately, these foods can lead to canine malnutrition, obesity, allergies, digestive problems, and pancreatitis. Certain meals even result in chemical burns to the mouth.

Here are some of the things that you should never give your dog:

Onions & garlic

While they add great taste to our food, onions and garlic are poisonous to dogs. No matter whether raw, cooked or dried - no dog should eat these. The essential oils contain sulfur substances that destroy the red blood cells of the four-legged friend. This leads to anemia, which in the worst case can be fatal.

Raw potatoes, eggplants & tomatoes

Some vegetables are unsuitable for dogs in their raw state. These include potatoes, eggplants (aubergines) and tomatoes, which belong to the nightshade family. All three contain the toxin solanine, which occurs mainly in the green areas. Raw or sprouting potatoes are particularly dangerous for dogs. It is also important to pour away the cooking water, as this is where the toxins collect. Overripe tomatoes without green spots are less harmful when raw.

Raw legumes

Uncooked legumes are harmful not just to dogs, but also to humans. Beans, peas, and other legumes are poisonous and inedible when raw because they include phasin, a neurotoxin. When eaten uncooked, the phasin inhibits protein synthesis in the small intestine and leads to blood cell clumping. Larger dosages can, in fact, be fatal.

Fruit cores

In general, cherries, peaches, or plums are safe for dogs to eat. However, be aware that the cores are hazardous. They contain the poison cyanide, which is converted into hydrogen cyanide in the stomach. As a result, the acid blocks cell division, the cells die and the dog suffocates internally. In addition, the risk of injury and clogging when swallowing the fruit kernels should not be ignored. So, remove the pips before feeding any fruit!

Avocado

Avocado is a great superfood for people, but it can be dangerous for dogs. Avocado flesh is indigestible for dogs, and swallowing the core has the potential to cause suffocation. There is still much to learn about the fruit and its effects on canines. Persin is a toxin present in some avocado varieties. This toxin can damage the heart muscle and ultimately even lead to the death of the dog. Since it is difficult to tell the poisonous from non-poisonous kinds, feeding should be avoided.

Raisins & grapes

Grapes and raisins are high in the toxin oxalic acid, which is harmful to dogs. This can cause kidney failure in certain breeds of dog, which might be fatal in the worst-case scenario. Small breeds, such as the Maltese or Yorkshire Terrier, can exhibit symptoms even after consuming tiny doses. You should avoid the fruit, even if you're sure your dog can eat it.

Chocolate, cocoa and tea

Chocolate and cocoa are poisonous for dogs. The theobromine in the items is toxic to dogs. The amount of theobromine in chocolate is usually higher in darker chocolates. A single overdose has the potential to cause heart failure and death in dogs. Tea and cocoa both include the substance.

Raw pork

Raw pork is not poisonous in itself, but eating it raw might cause Aujeszky's Disease infection. Although the virus is generally harmless to people, it can induce an incurable disease in dogs. The illness is characterized by inflammation of the nerves and brain, resulting in the animal's death. If you cook the meat for at least 60°C (140°F), germs will die and you can feed it without hesitation.

Walnuts & macadamia nuts

Walnuts are not poisonous to dogs, but the nut itself is indigestible. Fresh or unripe walnuts can be infected by a toxin-producing fungus. You cannot see it with the naked eye, but it harms your dog. It can cause symptoms such as tremors, convulsions, and even epileptic fits. Macadamia nuts are even toxic for dogs. In addition to a high content of unhealthy phosphorus, the nuts contain a toxin.

Alcohol

It should be well known that alcoholic beverages are unhealthy. However, the effects that the ethanol it contains on dogs are much stronger than on humans. Basically, it should be a matter of course for every pet owner that the animal roommates are not allowed to get alcohol. If your dog still takes a sip of alcohol, it can only break down the toxin slowly and incompletely. Just a few swallows are enough to kill a dog. You should also refrain from alcohol-free beer, as the hops it contains is also poisonous for dogs.

Beverages

Caffeine, as well as coffee, tea, soft drinks and other acidic beverages, can also cause chemical burns to the mouth. In addition, they can affect the nervous system and also cause breathing to stop.

04

Guidelines to Feed Your Dog

This chapter will teach you how to prepare your best friend's meals. You'll learn how much food your dog needs and when you should give more or less food.

Dogs are unique individuals, with different nutritional requirements depending on their age, size, breed, lifestyle, and physical exertion levels. How can you feed your four-legged friend so that they get exactly the right nutrients for their needs?

Small-breed puppies require a different quantity of energy and nutrients than larger-breed adults. Not only that, but certain breeds are more likely to suffer from specific health problems. Feeding your dog, the right diet is the best way to support their health and happiness.

This chapter will help you to clarify your dog's needs, taking into account their current stage of life and size, and to find the right nutrition for your dog.

Age Specific Diets

Your dog has different nutritional needs at different stages of their life. Puppies, for example, grow very quickly and need high-energy food to fuel this burst of growth, whereas older dogs slow their rate of growth and therefore need less energy.

Food for puppies and young dogs

A young pup's nutritional needs are different from those of a fully grown adult dog. Young pups need more protein and calcium in their diet as they grow. A diet that is well balanced will contribute to a pup's well-being and help them develop properly.

At the start, puppies are fed four to five times a day, but as they grow older, they are fed twice to three times a day. The amount of food provided varies by dog size and rises gradually with the animal's age. Under no circumstances should puppies be overfed. This can lead to rapid growth and problems with bone development. If your puppy is growing too fast, you should cut back on the amount of food and consult a veterinarian.

It is important to offer food that is both nutritious and tasty. Many puppies struggle with eating dry food, but you can add a little water or meat juice to it in order to make it more appetizing.

Puppies: The first six weeks

They should not be separated from the mother for the first six weeks of a dog's life. Breast milk is the best food for the puppy and strengthens its immune system against diseases. If circumstances have caused a separation from the mother, you can purchase milk supplements and bottles specially designed for puppies at any major pet store.

Puppies: Six weeks to six months

Puppies this age must be fed 3 to 4 times a day. Adequate nutrition is vital to your dog's growth and development. Puppies have different nutritional needs than adult dogs, so it is necessary to feed them a food specifically designed for puppies. Breed specific foods can provide a more specific diet for your pup. Large breed foods are especially important as they allow the puppy to grow at a rate that allows their bones and muscles to develop properly.

Check the ingredients of your feed to make sure it has adequate amounts of protein, calcium, and calories. When choosing a dog food, you should generally make sure that it does not contain any main components, that a wild dog would not eat. For example, avoid dog foods that have corn or by-products listed as the first ingredient.

Puppies: Six months to a year

From the age of six months, your puppy will only need two meals a day. The amount of food your dog needs depends on their size. Follow the instructions on the pack page and adjust the amount to suit your dog's needs. It is important not to overfeed. Your dog should be in healthy shape. The ribs should be felt but not seen, and your dog's waist should be visible from where you are.

Pick two times a day that your puppy will be fed regularly. It is important that feedings take place at a certain interval (e.g., in the morning and in the evening) so that the dog does not receive a meal for long periods of time.

One year old dogs

You should start switching your puppy to the adult food at one year of age. Any change in your dog's diet is important to be done slowly over a period of two or more weeks. Start by mixing small amounts of the new food with your dog's normal food. Every day, increase the amount of new forage and decrease the amount of the old one. Failure to mix the food for a long period of time can lead to stomach upset or food rejection.

Feeding your adult dog

Most dogs change their eating habits when they reach adulthood, but it is important that you don't change their diet too quickly. It may take a few days for your dog to get used to the new food, but after that, things should go smoother.

Adult dogs are usually fed once or twice a day. The size of the meal depends on the dog's size, but it should be enough to fill their stomach halfway. Large breeds may need more food than small breeds, but that does not mean that they should eat more frequently. A large breed that eats more than it needs, will end up overweight.

And of course, you still need to measure the amount your dog eats in order to make sure it doesn't become overweight. Make sure your dog isn't overfed while feeding, that it's acclimated to set feeding times, and that it can digest it in peace

Food for Senior dogs

When your dog is older and more sedentary, you can feed them a little less than usual. Older dogs experience changes in their bodies just like humans do and they need adapted and appropriate food and exercise. When determining how much to feed your dog, look at their physical condition rather than just their age. A healthy lifestyle will keep your dog young in many ways!

Older dogs generally have a reduced sense of taste and smell, so be aware that they may not favor the same types of food as before. You can use water to soften up dry food, which will help senior dogs, or consider using special food for geriatric or overweight dogs. This is a more delicate process for senior dogs, so be mindful of this when switching to a new food source.

What does this mean for your old dog's proper nutrition? The food of senior dogs should be wholesome and balanced. Antioxidants, for example, help support a healthy immune system.

In addition, older dogs can often no longer digest their food as well. Proper nutrition for senior dogs should therefore be based on food that is made with easily digestible ingredients that can be optimally used by the body. As older dogs can suffer from loss of appetite, it is important that they are fed a tasty dog food. A high protein content counteracts age-related muscle wasting. All of these and other factors play a role in properly feeding your senior dog.

Numerous vitamins and supplements are specifically targeted at older dogs, but you should try to fulfill your dog's needs with its diet first. Your veterinarian can help you determine which supplements or vitamins your dog may need.

Special Requirements

Some dogs have specific dietary needs, which you should take into account when choosing their food.

Small dog diet

Adult small breed dogs generally require a relatively high amount of energy, based on their size, meaning more calories per kilogram of body weight than large breed dogs. For proper nutrition, this means that you should prepare. A balanced diet ultimately ensures that adult small breed dogs receive all the nutrients that are important for them in this phase of life.

Proper nutrition for neutered dogs

If your four-legged friend has been neutered, there is a certain risk that he will become overweight. This may be because your dog is now showing more interest in eating and less interest in other dogs and the associated movement. Hormonal changes after neutering can also lead to obesity in dogs. Some dogs just feel calmer overall after the procedure. An interactive food bowl, in which the dog has to be playful for his meals, can keep him busy for longer times and increase his urge to move.

Food for dogs with health problems

If your dog has certain diseases or ailments, you should always check the food you are giving it with your veterinarian. For example, dog's suffering from diabetes should eat low glycemic index food. If your dog has problems with its teeth or jaw, you can feed it soft food that needs to be minced. Senior dogs and dogs with jaw problems may also need soft food.

If your dog has allergies, you should try to find out what foods are causing the reaction and avoid giving them those foods. Sometimes it helps to give your dog treats that are made of different ingredients.

Food for lactating dogs

Dogs that are nursing their young need more nutrients in order to produce milk. Their diet should consist of 20% more calories than normal. Lactating dogs need a lot of protein and calcium, so make sure you provide them with food that is rich in both. A lactating dog also needs more water. You should change their food gradually in order to avoid stomach problems, start by giving them 25% more food than normal and increase it depending on their needs.

Food for overweight dogs

If you are trying to lose weight yourself, you probably understand why you shouldn't eat in front of the TV or while you are working. The same goes for dogs. If you leave food down all day, your dog will think you're asking it to be constantly eating and will become overweight. Having a healthy lifestyle for your dog means creating good habits as well as making your dog feel comfortable.

Overweight dogs need to lose weight, and the best way to do this is by reducing their caloric intake. Start by giving them 30% less food than usual, and make sure they don't have access to food between meals. Your dog needs to move around more so you should walk it for at least 30 minutes a day and play with it.

You need to determine how much food your dog should eat throughout the day. The amount will depend on your dog's age, weight, and activity level. If you have a senior dog or a dog with other health problems, your veterinarian will recommend the best diet for it.

Food for dogs with diabetes

Dogs with diabetes have trouble metabolizing sugar, so they require diets that are low in carbohydrates. You have to be careful with insulin dosage because carbohydrates will affect it. They also need food that is high in fiber. This type of food is not made for other dogs, because even if they don't have diabetes, it can cause problems with their digestive systems. You shouldn't let your dog eat too many snacks between their regular meals.

Proper Nutrition for Sick Dogs

Does your dog have signs of wear and tear, infections, intolerance or other problems? Proper diet can alleviate symptoms and promote your dog's recovery. Make sure to consult your veterinarian before changing your dog's diet.

Diarrhea

Diarrhea occurs when the intestine is no longer able to draw water from food. There are many triggers for this reaction. Among other things, the disease can result from infections, parasites or food intolerance.

Before the feeding is adjusted, you should have the cause clarified by a veterinarian in order to counteract it with the right feed.

Acute diarrhea is usually an infection. Feeding rice with cooked chicken or cottage cheese can help your dog after a day of fasting. Charcoal tablets can also help alleviate symptoms.

Recurring diarrhea could mean an allergy or food intolerance. You can have a blood test, but only an elimination diet will give you an accurate result.

Constipation

Constipation is often caused by excessive bone-feeding as it hardens the feces. Other triggers are lack of exercise or water, as well as fur that was swallowed during grooming.

In this case, you can give your dog some milk or psyllium husks, which have a laxative effect. A high-fiber dog food is recommended for dogs that are more likely to suffer from constipation. If the constipation is persistent, a visit to the vet is essential.

Urinary stones

In addition to genetic predispositions, increased pH values in the urine, bladder infections or an oversupply of minerals are also causes of urinary stones.

Struvite and urate stones are the most common urinary stone images. These consist of salts of uric acid, a waste product of the DNA building block purine.

If your dog cannot break down purine properly for genetic reasons, it is best to use food with a lower protein content.

Leishmaniasis

This is a parasitic disease that can affect both dogs and masters. Often this occurs in the tropics and the Mediterranean area. Leishmaniasis is transmitted through the bite of sandflies and can manifest itself in the form of open wounds or fraying of the ears or damage to internal organs.

If your dog is sick, you should use a low protein diet and support the immune system.

Osteoarthritis

The excessive wear and tear of the joints can result from joint diseases, but also from pure wear and tear on the cartilage. The image of bone structures and stored connective tissue mean severe pain and reduced mobility for your dog.

In addition to physical therapy and medical measures, you should pay attention to your dog's weight. Osteoarthritis dogs should never be overweight. When choosing food, it is best to choose a low carb product.

The frequently made assumption that grain would promote osteoarthritis has not been confirmed, by the way!

Recommended Amount of Food

Obesity is becoming increasingly prevalent among dogs. Too much food is given to many dogs, and it's also served in low quality. Commercial food does not include specific feeding instructions. They're made for adult dogs that haven't been neutered as neutered dogs have lower metabolic rates and require less food. Furthermore, many dog owners do not measure out their dogs' portions, instead piling the dish high. Even worse, providing a dish of food that the dog may eat at any time during the day.

It's better to measure their food twice a day instead. (Unless you have a pup.) Every day, your dog should consume roughly 2.5 percent of his body weight, according to a typical rule. You'll increase or decrease this depending on your dog's activity level and whether you're attempting to maintain, lose weight, or gain weight.

Feeding guidelines by breed and weight

Important: This is just an indication for you to orientate. Adjust these amounts to your individual dog's needs!

Breed + average weight	Average daily serving
Chihuahua (6 pounds)	.2 pound per day (100g)
Shetland Sheepdog (20 pounds)	.5 pound per day (220g)
Dachshund (20–25 pounds)	.5–.625 pound per day (220g-280g)
Beagle (25 pounds)	.625 pound per day (280g)
Poodle (45–70 pounds)	1.125–1.75 pounds per day (500g-800g)
Bulldog (50 pounds)	1.25 pounds per day (570g)
Golden Retriever (60–80 pounds)	1.5–2 pounds per day (680g-900g)
Labrador Retriever (75 pounds)	1.875 pounds per day (850g)
German Shepherd (75–95 pounds)	1.875–2.25 pounds per day (850g-1000g)
Greyhound (80 pounds)	2 pounds per day (900g)
Rottweiler (90–110 pounds)	2.25–2.75 pounds per day (1000g-1250g)
Great Dane (120 pounds)	3 pounds per day (1350g)

How many calories does my dog need every day?

The type, amount and frequency of calories your dog consumes is determined by many factors, including his or her size and metabolism. Obesity may result from overfeeding your dog with excess energy. This can result in a variety of health problems. As a result, your dog's health requires that he or she get the correct quantity of appropriate food. A formula has been established by veterinarians to estimate the calorie requirements of your dog.

(Body weight of your dog in kilograms x 30) + 70 = RER *

* RER: The calculated value gives the calorie requirement per day without any activity.

To measure other factors are also important for the actual calorie requirement, the RER is multiplied by a factor that takes your dog's living situation into account:

- Adult, normally active dog, neutered: 1.6 x RER
- Adult, normally active dog, not neutered: 1.8 x RER
- Your dog does light work: 2 x RER
- Your dog does moderate work: 3 x RER
- Your dog does heavy work: 4-8 x RER
- Your dog is pregnant (<42 days): 1.8 x RER
- Your dog is pregnant (three weeks before the birth): 3 x RER
- Your dog is suckling puppies: 4-8 x RER (depending on how many puppies need to be looked after)
- Your puppy is younger than four months: 3 x RER
- Your dog is older than 4 months but not yet an adult: 2 x RER
- Your dog should lose weight: 1 x RER

As an example, let us calculate my own dog Max, a five-year-old mixed breed, 13 kilograms, neutered.

13 kg x30 + 70 = 460 calories (RER)
460 x 1.6 RER = 736 calories per day

According to this calculation, Max should be consuming 736 calories per day. To meet his demands, we must first know how many calories are in the daily diet.

05

How to Properly Set Up Your Kitchen

When preparing meals for your dog, you should make sure that all of your kitchen's supplies are in good shape. Learning how to cook for your dog will not only reward them with a nutritious meal each day, but will also give you a sense of accomplishment and make your bond even stronger.

Recommended Equipment

Although your home kitchen includes everything you need to prepare your dog's meals or treats, there are a few things that can make the process much easier if you decide to go with a homemade diet.

Storage containers

Containers for your dog's food must be well sealed to keep out pests, bacteria, and odors. Look for airtight plastic or glass containers that can be stacked, which will save space in your kitchen.

Cup measurements

If you are unfamiliar with using cups in recipes, you should get a cup measurement set. I have added a conversion chart in case you do not own this, but using the actual measurement makes life much easier in my opinion.

Freezer

A freezer is a valuable resource for premade meals and treats. If you're committed to preparing food on your own, freezing several batches of dog food and treats for later use is a good idea. Freezing the meals also helps to maximize their lifespan, eliminate freezer burn and maintain nutrients.

Electric food grinder

Using a food grinder, you may quickly prepare a suitable mixture of meat and vegetables. Grinding your own meat is far cheaper than buying ground meat, plus you can remove the fat for a healthier dinner. Although there are less expensive grinders available, only heavy-duty commercial grinders can grind bones. Grinding bones may void the warranty on even the costliest versions, so verify with the manufacturer before buying. You'll need to augment your dog's food if there's no bone in the meal.

Food dehydrator

Buying dried meats and vegetables is easy, but it's also pricey! Make your own dehydrated jerky and chews for a fraction of the price with a food dehydrator. Using a food dehydrator to dry vegetables and fruits for later use in meals is also a good idea during peak season.

Food scale

It's critical to measure your dog's food, both in terms of cups and weight, to ensure that you're feeding him the right amount of food every day. A food scale is a wise investment, as it will help you to accurately measure your dog's meals and maintain the proper weight.

Dog food dishes

You can purchase special ceramic or stainless-steel bowls for your dog to eat from, but you should also consider the size of your dog. Big dogs require big dishes, so if you have a large breed, buy the appropriately sized dishes for him or her. If you have several pets, use individual dishes so that each has their own food.

Store Food Properly

Food may be stored for a longer period of time if it is properly cared for. It can therefore be kept all year, regardless of the season or climate. There are various forms of storage that will protect and prolong the shelf life of your dog's food.

The primary reason for storing food at home is to have access to meals in the short, medium, and long term. Different food storage requirements exist for each type of food.

Food spoils as a result of physical, biochemical, chemical, and biological changes, as well as pest infestation. Bacteria, yeast, and mold are often the culprits behind spoilage. They make food rot, ferment or mold. Pathogenic microorganisms form substances that are harmful to humans - even without spoiling the food. The temperature, water activity, pH level and oxygen content of the food all influence how quickly germs multiply. The germ content of the food and the temperature at which it was stored are most significant.

Short-term storage: Refrigerator

Fresh, perishable food may be kept between 0°C (32°F) and 14°C (57°F). Food is kept at a temperature of 4°C (39°F) to 8°C (46°F) in a traditional refrigerator, and at almost 0°C (32°F) in a multi-zone refrigerator. Bacteria growth is slowed at these temperatures, and enzymatic and chemical spoilage is delayed. The ideal storage temperature in the refrigerator for most meals is close to the freezing point. Meat and fish can be stored at temperatures of around -2°C (28°F) for an extended time.

Basic rules for storage in the refrigerator:
- Fresh foods should be purchased as frequently as possible.
- When you're done shopping, store everything in the refrigerator as soon as possible. Always bring a cooler bag with you when going shopping!
- It's essential to keep your goods well-packed. The container prevents food from drying out and altering in taste.
- Place all of your food in the proper location: fish and meat at the bottom of the fridge, dairy products on top, cheese and leftovers on the top shelf, fruit and vegetables in the vegetable compartment.

This needs to be stored in the refrigerator: Meat and meat products, fish and fish products, prepared meals, milk and dairy products, cheese, drinks, butter, eggs, jams, dressings, sauces, tubes, refrigerator-compatible fruits and vegetables.

Medium-term storage: Freezer

Freezing food for many months provides a great way to save money and maintain nutrients, with little perceptible loss in quality. Low temperatures and reduced water activity help to prevent the multiplication of microorganisms. Keep in mind that microorganisms do not perish when frozen; rather, they resume reproducing after being defrosted. Biochemical changes such as fat oxidation or enzymatic breakdown processes are still taking place in the freezer but much slower. Fat becomes rancid even when frozen.

Freezer Rules to preserve the aroma, nutrients and quality
- Clean, wash, possibly peel and/or core, chop, blanch to maintain vitamins and color in fruits and vegetables before freezing.
-Freeze portions that are just right for consumption.
- Food should be packed as airtight as possible.
- Make labels with the name and date of the contents.
- Frozen food does not have an infinite shelf life: fruit and vegetables 11 to 15 months, beef and poultry 9 to 12 months, fish and high-fat meat 6 to 9 months.

These should not be stored in the freezer: Eggs, lettuce, fresh salad, radishes, raw potatoes, cucumbers, tomatoes, watermelons, whole raw apples and pears. When frozen, water-rich foods become mushy. Also, dairy products should not be kept in the freezer.

Long-term storage: Pantry

Preserved and dry food can be stored long-term in pantries at an average of 15°C (59°F) to 20°C (68°F), in a dry and dark place. A pantry should be located as close to the kitchen as possible and have good ventilation.

Because of the temperature and generally high humidity, the kitchen is not a great storage area. Only supplies that are quickly consumed should be kept here. In apartment complexes, however, it is usually the only location to keep food.

Careful storage and regular maintenance reduce storage losses and spoilage:
- If a food item has an expiration date, check it before opening or consuming it.
- Always put new supplies to the back of the shelf, use up the oldest first.
- Transfer opened packages into tightly fitting containers made of glass, metal or plastic.
- Label preserved food with name and date.
- Do not consume food from a can (tin) with a bulging bottom or lid, or if a jar is no longer airtight

Store in storage cupboards: preserved food, flour, salt, sugar, whole canned (tinned) foods, dry products such as rice, pasta or cereals.

Tips to Start

When starting out with cooking for your dog, it can be a bit daunting, but don't worry. Getting started is always the hardest part, and while there's a lot of information to take in, it's not all that hard. The following tips can help you get started.

When you're just getting started, it's a good idea to try out one recipe at a time. Making small changes in your dog's diet is a lot easier on your dog than switching to a whole new diet all at once.

You can start slow; it is not all or nothing. Actually, some healthy food is better than none at all. And it doesn't matter what you started with because any change is good.

Don't be discouraged if your dog rejects the new food or takes a little time to get used to it. Some changes your dog may reject at first, but as he gets used to tasting new food, you'll find that he or she actually comes to enjoy it.

Start small and build up! The more you cook, the better you will get at it. Find your rhythm and extend the types of meals you cook.

Preparation is key. Be sure to prepare ahead of time. Always read the recipe from start to finish, and get all ingredients measured out in advance. Make sure that you have everything you need to make the meal, and that you understand what each ingredient does.

Cook ahead of time and store your dog's food. Always cook more than you need, and save the extra portions in the freezer. Having healthy meals ready to warm up saves you time and money.

There's no need to feel like a short order cook. If your dog doesn't like a certain type of food, try another recipe with a similar ingredient until you find one, they do like. It may help you to mix the new food with his old food, or just introduce the new one gradually.

If you're starting with a homemade diet, it's smart to consult a veterinarian before you start your dog on it. They'll be able to give you the proper nutritional information for a homemade diet and will let you know if you're feeding your dog correctly.

It's also a good idea to stick to the recipe and not improvise at first. Getting used to a new diet can be hard on your dog, and they may end up rejecting the food. If this happens, try adding some things back in, but cut out the more exotic ingredients.

06

Breakfast Dishes

The early hours are a favorite part of our dogs' days, for them getting up early and patrolling the garden before coming in for breakfast. Of course, this implies we'll have to get up early as well. Many of these dog breakfasts may be prepared ahead of time and enjoyed right away, which is convenient. In fact, we occasionally employ the same strategy for our own meals by preparing breakfast that may be reheated quickly. A delicious breakfast is an excellent way to start your dog's day with nutritious options, and it's a wonderful bonding opportunity!

Mini Quiche with Liver

This dish is based on chicken liver and eggs, both of which are reasonably priced. This dish may be prepared in advance and stored in the refrigerator for several days, which makes it very convenient.

Preparation time: 15 minutes

Cooking time: 30 minutes

Quantity: 6 muffins or more

3 eggs • ¼ lb. (110g) chicken livers, washed and cooked • ¼ cup cooked green beans, chopped

1. Preheat the oven to 350°F (180°C). Fill muffin tins with parchment paper or grease them.

2. With the back of a fork, mash chicken livers until they're smooth. Use a knife for any big pieces. In a mixing bowl, whisk the eggs, then add the chicken livers and green beans.

3. Fill muffin pans three-quarters full with batter and bake for 30 minutes, or until golden brown, depending on the size of the muffins.

Spinach Omelet

Isn't it wonderful to have an omelet for breakfast? Green leafy vegetables, particularly spinach, are a fantastic choice since they offer both color and nutrients.

Preparation time: 10 minutes

Cooking time: 5 minutes

Quantity: 36 treats

1 egg • 1 cup torn baby spinach leaves • 1 tbsp Parmesan cheese, grated

1. In a small mixing dish, beat the eggs, then add the spinach and cheese. Over medium-high heat, warm some oil in a pan

2. Cook for 5 minutes until partially cooked, then turn with a spatula to finish to desired consistency.

3. Allow to cool. Refrigerate any leftovers for up to 3 days.

Deviled Eggs

Deviled eggs are a must-have at our family gatherings. For extra taste and nutrients, chicken livers are included to this dog food. My dogs love it and devour quickly.

Preparation time: 40 minutes

Cooking time: 20 minutes

Quantity: 12 half-eggs

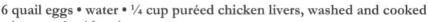

6 quail eggs • water • ¼ cup puréed chicken livers, washed and cooked • 1 tsp apple cider vinegar

1. Place the whole eggs in a pot, cover with water, and cook until they start to boil. Cover the pan, lower the heat to low, and cook for 1 minute longer.

2. Remove the eggs from the heat and set them aside for 15 minutes, covered. Remove and rinse the eggs for 1 minute in cool water.

3. Crack and peel eggs while they're under running water.

4. Remove the yolks from the eggs by cutting them in half lengthwise and placing them in a medium mixing bowl. In a separate mixing dish, combine the chicken liver purée and apple cider vinegar. To make a delicious crumble, combine the yolks, chicken livers, and vinegar in a mixing bowl.

5. Stir in the egg yolk mixture to the bowl with the eggs.

Cottage Cheese Breakfast

A good-tasting morning meal that can be served to your dog or kept for yourself to get you started off on the right foot!

Preparation time: 5 minutes

Quantity: 1 cup

⅓ cup of cottage cheese • ⅓ cup of plain yogurt • ⅓ cup blueberries, mashed

1. In a medium bowl, combine all of the ingredients.

2. This meal can be stored in the fridge for up to 5 days.

Fishermen's Eggs

Greetings, mateys! When it's time to eat, even landlubber dogs will be happy to chow down on this seafood-inspired dinner.

Preparation time: 10 minutes
Cooking time: 15 minutes
Quantity: 2 cups

1 sardine can (3.75 oz./100g) in water • 2 tbsp parsley • 4 quail eggs

1. Preheat the oven to 350°F (180°C). Grease an 8" casserole.

2. Drain the sardines, then save the water for another meal or a delicious dog Food Topping. Combine the chopped sardines and parsley.

3. Place the sardine mix in the prepared casserole, followed by the eggs. Crack the individual eggs and distribute them throughout the dish, or whip the eggs and pour them over the sardines.

4. Bake for 15 minutes, or until your preferred degree of doneness is achieved.

Baked Eggs Muffins

These wonderful, protein-rich muffins are a great way to begin Penny's Day, they are quick to prepare and they'll be appreciated at any time.

Preparation time: 15 minutes
Cooking time: 30 minutes
Quantity: 16 small muffins

12 eggs • ½ cup of cotton cheese • ½ tsp powdered baking soda • 1 cup Cheddar cheese, shredded • ½ cup cooked shredded chicken • 1 can tuna (5 oz./140g) in water, drained

1. Preheat the oven to 350°F (180°C). Fill muffin tins (small size) with parchment paper or grease them.

2. In a big mixing bowl, whisk together the eggs, cottage cheese, baking soda, cheese, chicken, and tuna.

3. Fill each cup with the egg mixture and bake for 30 minutes, until firm.

Chia Seed Oatmeal

Do you want to make a nutritious breakfast for yourself and your dog? The night before, prepare the dish and refrigerate it overnight. You'll be treated to a delicious breakfast prepared with chia, a superfood high in omega-3 fatty acids, calcium, and other nutrients.

Preparation time: 20 minutes
Quantity: 4 cups

1 cup almond milk • 1 cup unsweetened oats • 2 apples • 2 tsp chia seeds • 2 tbsp honey • 1 tsp lemon extract • 1 cup plain Greek yogurt (low-fat)

1. In a mixing bowl, combine the almond milk and oats and chia seeds.

2. After removing the core, mix the grated apples, honey, and lemon juice. Make certain that the apple seeds don't come into contact with your dog's mouth. Combine the chia seed and oats with the apples and yogurt.

3. Combine all ingredients in a large mixing bowl and thoroughly mix. Cover and chill overnight. To make sure the chia seeds are ready, let them sit for at least 12 hours. Store for up to five days in the refrigerator.

Raw Breakfast

With this basic breakfast, you may get your day off to a good start without spending too much time in the kitchen. This dish can feed a 30- to 40-pound dog in one sitting.

Preparation time: 10 minutes
Quantity: 2cups

1 egg • 1 washed chicken liver • 4oz (110g) of flesh (muscle or heart) • ½ tsp apple cider vinegar • 3 tbsp simple yogurt, cottage cheese, or kefir • 1 tsp flaxseed seed oil • ½ tsp honey

1. In a large mixing bowl, crack an egg and break up the eggshell into small pieces.

2. Before serving, combine the chicken liver and muscle meat with the apple cider vinegar, yogurt, flaxseed oil, and honey.

07

Main Dishes

Would you like to offer a special meal for your dog? Your small buddy will enjoy the delicious ingredients, which include hefty, fishy, and vegetarian dishes. I've included a variety of classic, raw, Paleo, and grain-free recipes in this book. You may try all of these recipes if you want to provide variety and keep your mind open. Make sure your dog eats the meal before offering treats.

Rice with Beef

If you're in the mood for a substantial dinner, this is one not to miss. It's ideal for sharing with your dog. Simply add some hot pepper sauce to your portion and leave your dog's portion dog friendly.

Preparation time: 20 minutes

Cooking time: 40 minutes

Quantity: 6-7cups

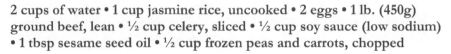

2 cups of water • 1 cup jasmine rice, uncooked • 2 eggs • 1 lb. (450g) ground beef, lean • ½ cup celery, sliced • ½ cup soy sauce (low sodium) • 1 tbsp sesame seed oil • ½ cup frozen peas and carrots, chopped

1. Bring a saucepan of water to a boil over high heat. Add the rice and cook as directed on the package. Typically, this should last for 18–25 minutes, or until cooked and the liquid has been absorbed.

2. Whisk the eggs in a small dish. Pour them into a skillet and simmer until firm.

3.. Remove from the heat and cut the eggs into strips, then return the skillet to the stove.

4. In a skillet over medium heat, cook the ground beef and celery until the beef is thoroughly cooked. This should take about 10 minutes.

5. Combine the soy sauce and sesame oil in a small bowl and then add to the meat. Add cooked rice, carrots and peas, and cooked egg strips to the pan. Cook for 3–4 minutes, or until everything is completely combined and heated through.

6. If you're feeding both dogs and people, add some extra flavorings to your own dish.

Buffalo Meatballs

It's always fascinating to see how dogs react to new flavors. When we first served bison rather than beef, Max and Penny were hesitant. It subsequently became a runaway success! Buffalo meat is very lean and full of protein, so it's a great choice for dogs.

Preparation time: 25 minutes

Cooking time: 10 minutes

Quantity: 30 meatballs

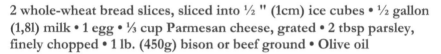

2 whole-wheat bread slices, sliced into ½ " (1cm) ice cubes • ½ gallon (1,8l) milk • 1 egg • ⅓ cup Parmesan cheese, grated • 2 tbsp parsley, finely chopped • 1 lb. (450g) bison or beef ground • Olive oil

1. In a medium bowl, soak bread cubes in milk for about 5 minutes. Remove the bread from the milk, press out any excess liquid, and discard the milk.

2. Combine the bread, egg, cheese, parsley, and bison. Using your fingers, form little balls out of the mixture.

3. In a large saucepan over medium-high heat, cook the meatballs for 8–10 minutes or until no longer pink in the center.

Buffalo Hash

Buffalo has a lower fat level and half the cholesterol of beef. If you don't have ground buffalo on hand, this simple dish may be made using ground beef, chicken, or turkey.

Preparation time: 10 minutes

Cooking time: 25 minutes

Quantity: 7 cups

2 tbsp olive oil • 1 lb. (450g) buffalo meat • 2 eggs • 2 cups chopped frozen veggies (without onion and garlic) • 2 cups brown rice, cooked

1. Cook the rice as directed on the package.

2. In the meantime, place the ground buffalo in a large skillet and cook for 10 minutes, or until no longer pink on the inside.

3. Add the eggs, chopped vegetables, and brown rice to the skillet. Reduce the heat to medium and cook for about 10 minutes.

Meal of Mutt Meatloaf

This entire meal may be assembled ahead of time to feed your dog for multiple days. It's also a great one to cook in bulk if you have a large dog or multiple pooches. Simply increase and double, triple, or even quadruple the portions as necessary.

Preparation time: 10 minutes

Cooking time: 60 minutes

Quantity: 16 cups

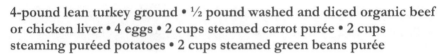

4-pound lean turkey ground • ½ pound washed and diced organic beef or chicken liver • 4 eggs • 2 cups steamed carrot purée • 2 cups steaming puréed potatoes • 2 cups steamed green beans purée

1. Preheat the oven to 350°F (180°C).

2. Combine the ingredients in a large mixing bowl and fill into a baking dish. Place the pan in an oven and bake for one hour.

Rice with Beef and Fish

This dish was a cinch to produce, and contains both beef and fish. It's also one of the most popular recipes of Max.

Preparation time: 20 minutes

Cooking time: 30 minutes

Quantity: 8 servings

4 lbs. (1800g) ground beef • 1 sweet potato • 3 cups cooked white rice • 1 can of mackerel, drained • 4 cups peas & carrots • 6 eggs • 6 egg shells • 1 tbsp rosemary, finely chopped • 1 tbsp ginger, finely chopped

1. Preheat the oven to 350°F (180°C). Brown the ground beef in a pan and drain all of the grease.

2. Pierce sweet potato with a fork and microwave for 10 minutes or until soft.

3. Bake eggs shells in the oven for 10 minutes, when done blend or mash until they form a powder.

4. Steam veggies and then mash with the rosemary and ginger.

5. Add all ingredients into the pan and heat all ingredients.

Lamb with Veggies

Lamb is one of those meals that has our dogs' ears perking up. Yes, they are aware of the meaning of the term lamb.

Preparation time: 10 minutes

Cooking time: 25 minutes

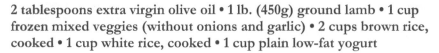

Quantity: 7 cups

2 tablespoons extra virgin olive oil • 1 lb. (450g) ground lamb • 1 cup frozen mixed veggies (without onions and garlic) • 2 cups brown rice, cooked • 1 cup white rice, cooked • 1 cup plain low-fat yogurt

1. Cook the rice as directed on the package.

2. In a large pan over medium-high heat, warm the olive oil. Cook the ground lamb for 10 minutes or until the meat is no longer pink.

3. Add the frozen vegetables to the skillet and simmer for another 15 minutes.

4. Combine the ground beef, rice, and yogurt in a large mixing basin once cool.

Fruity Chicken Soup

Preparation time: 30 minutes

Cooking time: 3 hours

Quantity: 10 servings

3-pound (1300g) roasting chicken, quartered • 2 quarts (liters) water • 1 1/2 cups homemade chicken broth • 2 cups chopped celery • 2 cups chopped carrots • 2 large apples, chopped • 1 cup chopped green beans • 1/4 cup chopped fresh parsley • 4 cups uncooked egg noodles

1. Place the chicken and water in a large stockpot and simmer for 2 1/2 hours.

2. After cooking, remove the chicken from the pot and allow it to cool. Remove the skin and bones before shredding the meat into small pieces by pulling it apart with your hands. Return the meat to the pot with the broth.

3. Add the chicken broth, celery, carrots, apples, green beans, and parsley and simmer for 25 minutes.

4. Add the noodles and cook for 8 to 10 minutes until the noodles are tender.

Scotch Eggs

Here's a beloved British cuisine that you and your dog may enjoy.

Preparation time: 40 minutes

Cooking time: 40 minutes

Quantity: 15 treats

4 eggs • 1 lb. (450g) mild ground pork sausage • 3 tbsp all-purpose flour ¾ cup panko bread crumbs • 4 hard-boiled eggs • 1 egg, beaten

1. Preheat the oven to 400°F (205°C).

2. Make four patties from the ground sausage. Fill a small basin halfway with bread crumbs. In a separate bowl, sift the flour. In a third bowl, beat the egg.

3. Roll each hard-boiled egg in flour to coat it. Place the eggs on the sausage patties and mold the sausage to fit around it.

4. Take a sausage-covered egg, dip it in the beaten egg, and then in the bread crumbs until completely coated.

5. Bake the covered sausage-egg for 30–40 minutes, or until fully cooked.

Bean Soup

Preparation time: 30 minutes

Cooking time: 4 hours

Quantity: 10 servings

3½ quarts (liters) water • 2 whole tomatoes • 1 pound (450g / 2 cups) dried navy beans • 1 meaty ham bone (1 ½ pounds / 600g) • 1 cup cubed potatoes • 1 cup thinly sliced celery • 1 cup chopped carrots

1. In a saucepan, bring water to a boil. Cook the tomatoes for 3 minutes before putting them in cold water. Remove the tomato skins. Dice the tomatoes.

2. Bring 2 ½ quarts (liters) water to a boil., cook beans for 2 minutes.

3. Add the ham bone to the beans and simmer for 2 hours, or until almost soft.

4. Add the potatoes, celery, carrots, blanched tomatoes and simmer for 1 hour.

5. Remove the ham bone and cut away the flesh, dice it, and add it to the beans.

Stomach-friendly Chicken and Rice

A simple supper is ideal for dogs who are recovering from an upset stomach.

Preparation time: 10 minutes

Cooking time: 90 minutes

Quantity: 6 cups

2 chicken breasts • 2 quarts (liters) of water • 1 cup rice, white

1. Remove the bones, fat, and skin from the chicken breasts.

2. Bring the water to a boil. Cook chicken breasts about 30 minutes.

3. Remove the chicken from the water and add the rice to the pot. Set the heat to medium and simmer for about 30 minutes. Cook until the rice is soft but not overcooked. While the rice cooks, shred the chicken using two forks.

4. Remove the pan from the heat and let it cool. After 30 minutes, drain off some of the remaining water, but keep the mixture moist and soupy.

5. Return the chicken to the pot and allow to cool completely before serving.

Chicken Meatloaf

Meatloaves are easy to prepare and freeze, and you may cook in bulk by increasing the recipe.

Preparation time: 20 minutes

Cooking time: 105 minutes

Quantity: 8 cups

½ cup barley • 4 cup chicken broth • 1 ½lb (680g) ground chicken • ½ cup cottage cheese (low-fat) • 2 eggs, whole • ½ cup oats, rolled • ¾ cup carrots, finely chopped • 1 tbsp olive oil

1. Bring the barley and chicken stock to a boil in a medium saucepan, then reduce the heat and simmer for 45 minutes. Let it cool down a bit.

2. Preheat the oven to 350°F (180°C). Grease 9" x 13" (23x33cm) baking dish.

3. Combine ground chicken, cottage cheese, eggs, rolled oats, carrots, and olive oil. Combine well. In a slow, steady stream, add the cooled barley and liquid.

4. Bake for 1 hour after putting the ingredients in the pan.

Pumpkin with Stuffing

This multi-meal one-dish recipe combines some of Max's healthiest fall favorites into one simple-to-prepare dish.

Preparation time: 20 minutes

Cooking time: 60 minutes

Quantity: 6 cups

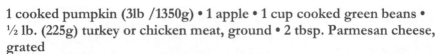

1 cooked pumpkin (3lb /1350g) • 1 apple • 1 cup cooked green beans • ½ lb. (225g) turkey or chicken meat, ground • 2 tbsp. Parmesan cheese, grated

1. Preheat the oven to 350°F (180°C).

2. Remove the pumpkin's top and scoop out all of the seeds with a spoon.

3. Remove the core and seeds from the apple, then thinly slice it. Green beans should be chopped into small pieces.

4. In a mixing bowl, combine green beans, apple, turkey, and Parmesan cheese. Stuff the pumpkin until it is completely full.

5. Place the pumpkin, cut side up on a baking tray and bake for 1 hour. Remove any liquid from the top of the pumpkin while it cooks.

6. Allow it to cool fully before serving. To eat, cut the pumpkin in half, scoop out the stuffing and flesh from the inside, then scrape out the rest of the pumpkin.

7. Refrigerate leftovers for up to 3 days or freeze for up to 3 months in an airtight container.

Chicken and Pumpkin Casserole

Preparation time: 20 minutes

Cooking time: 50 minutes

Quantity: 10 servings

2 chicken breasts • 1 cup cooked rice • 1 cup frozen peas • 1 celery stock, cut into small pieces • 1 cup pumpkin puree • 1 boiled potato, cut into bite-size pieces • 3 tbsp homemade chicken broth

1. Preheat the oven to 350°F (180°C). Remove the skin from the chicken breasts and cut them into bite-size pieces.

2. Place the chicken breasts in a saucepan with just enough water to cover them. Bring to a boil, then reduce heat and simmer for 30 minutes or until cooked through.

3. Add all of the ingredients to a large mixing dish and combine thoroughly. Pour into a casserole dish and bake for 20 minutes.

Shepherd's Pie

Preparation time: 40 minutes

Cooking time: 25 minutes

Quantity: 9 cups

2 big potatoes • 1 big sweet potato, medium • 1 lb. (450g) cooked chicken (any cut)
½ lb. (225g) cooked chicken heart • ¼ cup homemade chicken broth • 4 tbsp melted bacon fat (optional) • 1 cup carrots, shredded • 2 celery stalks, minced • 1 cup cottage cheese (low-fat)

1. Preheat the oven to 350°F (180°C).

2. Peel and quarter the potatoes, then boil until soft.

3. Finely chop the chicken and chicken hearts and combine with chicken broth and bacon fat (if using) in a large mixing bowl. In a 9" x 13" (23x33cm) baking dish, layer the carrots and celery. Add the cottage cheese on top.

4. Spread potatoes on top of the casserole with a fork. Bake for 40 minutes..

Penny's Flautas

Preparation time: 40 minutes

Cooking time: 25 minutes

Quantity: 9 flautas

1 lb. (450g) chicken breasts cooked and deboned • 1 cup drained cooked black beans (canned) • 9 flour tortillas (whole wheat) • ½ cup shredded cheese Monterey jack or cheddar cheese

1. Preheat the oven to 350°F (180°C). Lightly grease a baking tray.

2. Shred the chicken with two forks. With a fork, mash the black beans.

3. Spread a little layer of black beans on each tortilla before adding the shredded chicken and cheese. Tuck it in tightly with a toothpick.

4. Arrange flautas on a baking tray and bake for 20 minutes.

Sardine Cake

Sardines are high in omega-3 and -6 fatty acids, making them a superfood. It's a genuine dog-friendly component that your dog will love!

Preparation time: 40 minutes

Cooking time: 25 minutes

Quantity: 6-9

2 sweet potatoes • 2 cans (3.75 oz./100g) sardines in water, drained and chopped • 1 beaten egg • 2 tbsp all-purpose flour • ½ cup panko bread crumbs • 2 tbsp olive oil

1. Place the sweet potatoes in a pot, cover with water, and cook until soft.

2. Mash the sweet potatoes after peeling away the skins. In a mixing dish, combine the sardines, egg, and flour. Stir in 1 cup bread crumbs completely.

3. Form three tiny burger patties from the dough; you may also try making them triangular. The leftover bread crumbs should be used to coat the patties.

4. In a large saucepan, heat 2 tablespoons olive oil over medium-high heat. Sauté the sardine patties in batches of two or three until golden brown, flipping halfway through.

Salmon Balls

Salmon is a great source of omega-3 fatty acids, so add it to your dog's diet and watch his or her coat gleam. You should use only fresh fish, not canned.

Preparation time: 20 minutes

Cooking time: 15 minutes

Quantity: 12 balls

1 cup cooked brown rice • 1 ½ cup cooked salmon, diced • 1 egg • 1 tbsp of extra virgin olive oil

1. Preheat the oven to 350°F (180°C). Grease a baking tray.

2. In a medium mixing bowl, fully combine all ingredients. With a spoon, scoop the mixture and roll into 12 balls. Place on the baking tray and bake it in the oven for 15 minutes.

4. Allow to cool fully before giving it to your dog. Freeze for up to 6 months in an airtight container, or keep it for 3 days in the refrigerator.

Salmon and Spinach Hash

One-dish meals are ideal for both our pets and ourselves since they're convenient. This dinner may be simple, but it's jam-packed with nutrients!

Preparation time: 5 minutes

Cooking time: 20 minutes

Quantity: 4 cups

1 tsp extra virgin olive oil • 1 cup thawed frozen spinach • 1 (7.5-ounce/210g) tin salmon, drained • 4 quail eggs

1. In a medium saucepan, heat the olive oil over medium-high heat. Add the fish and spinach and continue to cook until they are fully cooked.

2. Scramble the eggs and add them to the pan.

3. Allow to cool. Refrigerate for up to 3 days before serving.

Tuna Pasta

Tuna Pasta is a fine dish to share with your dog. In your own portion, use some mayonnaise.

Preparation time: 10 minutes

Cooking time: 10 minutes

Quantity: 2 cups

Tuna in a can (9 oz./260g) packed with water • 1 cup drained cooked pasta • ½ cup thawed frozen peas • ¼ cup fresh parsley, chopped • ¼ cup Parmesan cheese, grated

1. Cook pasta of your choice according to package instructions. Use warm pasta for yourself, but let it cool for your dog.

2. Drain the tuna and save the water to use in a treat recipe instead of water.

3. In a large mixing basin, combine the tuna, pasta, peas, parsley, and cheese.

Max and Penny's Spinach

Popeye's favorite muscle food, when eaten in moderation, is also wonderful for dogs. Spinach is high in vitamins and includes lutein. Lutein is an antioxidant that promotes healthy eyes and vision.

Preparation time: 20 minutes

Cooking time: 25 minutes

Quantity: 6 cups

2 large eggs • 2 tablespoons extra virgin olive oil • 2 cups cooked brown rice • 2 cup fresh sprouting spinach • 1 can drained and chopped sprats (8.5oz/240g)

1. Cook the rice and cook as directed on the package.

2. In a mixing cup, smash the eggs with a fork. Cook the eggs in a pan over medium heat until firm. Remove the pan from the heat.

3. After removing the eggs from the pan, cut them into thin strips.

4. In a skillet, combine the rice and olive oil over medium heat. Stir constantly until the rice is heated, then add the spinach. Cover and simmer until the spinach is completely cooked. Stir in the sprats and eggs until well combined.

56

Spaghetti Squash with Veggies

This grain-free cuisine is suitable for sharing with your four-legged companions. It contains rich, hearty flavors that will have your dog begging for more.

Preparation time: 20 minutes

Cooking time: 40 minutes

Quantity: 3 cups

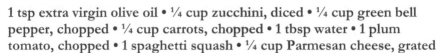

1 tsp extra virgin olive oil • ¼ cup zucchini, diced • ¼ cup green bell pepper, chopped • ¼ cup carrots, chopped • 1 tbsp water • 1 plum tomato, chopped • 1 spaghetti squash • ¼ cup Parmesan cheese, grated

1. Preheat the oven to 350°F (180°C).

2. Cut in half lengthwise and scoop out the seeds. Place on a baking tray, flesh side up.

3. Bake for 30–40 minutes or until easily pierced with a fork. Allow to cool before handling.

4. Remove the flesh with a fork and discard the skin. Place cooked squash in a large mixing bowl and set aside.

5. In a large skillet over medium heat, cook the zucchini, bell pepper, and carrots for 5-10 minutes.

6. Cook for a further 5 minutes after adding the tomato and water.

7. Serve over spaghetti squash with cheese on top.

8. Before serving the dog's portion, allow to cool to room temperature. Refrigerate for up to 5 days or freeze for up to 6 months in an airtight container.

Pumpkin Rice

While on vacation in Jamaica, we first came upon pumpkin rice. This dog-friendly recipe does not contain the typical spices or Scotch Bonnet peppers.

Preparation time: 10 minutes

Cooking time: 20 minutes

Quantity: 5 cups

1 tbsp olive oil • 1 cup frozen mixed veggies (without onions and garlic) • 1 cup pureed pumpkin • 2 cups broth (chicken or veggie) • 2 cups instant brown rice, uncooked

1. In a large saucepan, bring the vegetables, Pumpkin Purée, and water to a boil. Stir once or twice while it cooks.

2. Add the rice to the saucepan and return to a boil over medium heat. Reduce the temperature to low and cook for another 5 minutes.

3. Remove from heat and set aside for 10 minutes, until the rice and veggies have absorbed all of the liquid. Refrigerate for 3–4 days

Oat Mix

This dish may be prepared in advance and kept in the fridge. Simply add hot water like you would with a fresh batch.

Preparation time: 5 minutes

Cooking time: 30 minutes

Quantity: 2 cups

1 cup oats • ¼ cup smashed, cooked pinto beans • ¼ cup wheat bran • 1 tbs. soy lecithin • 1 tbs. wheat germ • 1 tbs. ground sunflower seeds • 1/6 tbs. molasses • 1 tsp. ground flax seed • ½ tbs. olive oil

1. Combine all of the ingredients in a mixing bowl and soak in hot water for approximately 30 minutes.

Raw Beef

This is a simple recipe for raw beef. The eggshells enhance the calcium content.

Preparation time: 10 minutes

Quantity: 4 cups

1 lb. (450g) raw ground beef • 2 hardboiled eggs with shells • 2 cups cooked white rice

1. Cut the hard-boiled eggs into small pieces, including the shells.

2. Combine with white rice and ground beef to make a hearty meal.

3. Refrigerate for up to 2 days or freeze for up to 6 months in an airtight container.

Raw Organ Mix

Easy recipe for a nutritious raw mix. Organ meat is a rich source of nutrients

Preparation time: 10 minutes

Quantity: 4 cups

1 lb. (450g) raw meat of choice (beef or chicken) • 2 ounces organ meats and fat (liver, gizzards, necks, backs, feet, tails, tongue) • 1 cup carrots, pureed • 1 cup spinach or broccoli pureed • ½ cup apple cider vinegar • ½ cup plain yogurt • 3 eggs with shells finely ground • ¼ cup parsley

1. Mix all ingredients together

2. Refrigerate for up to 2 days or freeze for up to 6 months in an airtight container.

Raw Meatloaf

This simple raw loaf recipe may be made with whatever meat and veggies are readily available at your local market. Meatloaf is a wonderful method to utilize up seasonal items while also providing enough variety for your dog to never get bored with his or her meals.

Preparation time: 15 minutes

Quantity: 6 cups

1 lb. (450g) beef, bison, lamb, turkey, or chicken, raw • 2 cups veggies puréed • ¼ cup washed liver, gizzards, or kidneys • ½ cup apple cider vinegar • ½ cup plain low-fat yogurt • 3 shelled eggs, finely broken

1. In a large mixing basin, combine all of the ingredients.

2. Refrigerate for 2 days or freeze for up to 6 months in an airtight container.

Raw Chicken Dinner

You can offer this chicken meal boneless, with finely ground bones, or with whole bones, depending on your dog's eating habits. Some raw feeders offer their dogs with edible bones as part of the diet or after grinding them. Bones are high in key nutrients.

Preparation time: 10 minutes

Quantity: 3 cups

1 lb. (450g) chopped raw chicken • ½ lb. (225g) chicken livers, whole, washed, and cut • 1 egg • 2 tablespoons plain low-fat yogurt • 1 tsp honey • 1 tbsp apple cider vinegar • ¼ tsp of flaxseed oil • 1 tsp powdered kelp seaweed • 1 tsp powdered alfalfa

1. Place all of the ingredients in a large mixing dish and combine them with a spoon. Then serve the meal in proportion to your dog's size.

2. Refrigerate for 2 days or freeze for up to 6 months in an airtight container.

08

Slow cooker recipes

In this chapter we will share recipes for your electric cooker. These dishes are the easiest and the least time-consuming to prepare, and on top they all taste delicious!

If you do not own an electric cooker and haven't tried one, now is the time! They are very easy to use and so convenient!

I prefer the setting low, but if you are in a rush, you may use high and half the time.

Slow Beef

There's no reason why you can't make it once a week with this dish being so easy. You may put all of your ingredients in the slow cooker in the morning and forget about it until dinnertime. It's not possible to overcook the food since it's fine if it gets mushy. That's what makes this dish so ideal for people who are very busy with work or family life.

Preparation time: 10 minutes

Cooking time: 6 hours

Quantity: 9 cups

2 ½ lb. (1100g) beef (ground) • 1 (15 oz./420g) can washed and drained kidney beans • 1 ½ cup brown rice • 1 ½ cups butternut squash, peeled and cut into small cubes • 1 ½ cups finely chopped carrots • ¾ cup fresh or frozen peas

1. In a slow cooker, combine ground beef, rice, beans, squash, carrots, peas.

2. Pour in 4 cups of water and mix everything.

3. Cook on low for 6 hours or more in your slow cooker.

Basic Rice and Beef

This basic dish is a recipe that may be customized in a variety of ways. Substitute different meats, vegetables and seasonings for a whole new dish that fits your furry family's preferences.

Preparation time: 20 minutes

Cooking time: 8 hours

Quantity: 6 cups

1 lb. (450g) ground beef • 1 cup frozen vegetables • 1 cup white rice • 1 c pearl barley • 1 apple or pear (cored and chopped) • water

1. In a mixing bowl, combine all of the ingredients and gradually add 3 quarts (liters) of water.

2. Add about two tablespoons each of 3 herbs (Herbs: basil, dill, coriander, oregano, parsley, sage, spearmint, tarragon, thyme)

3. Add 1 tablespoon of spice (cinnamon, cumin, nutmeg, ginger or allspice)

4. Cook on low for 8 hours

Slow Turkey

Make your dog's meals from scratch. It's simpler than ever to make delicious food with a slow cooker. In this simple slow cooker dog food recipe, turkey and a variety of veggies, such as carrots, sweet potatoes, and green beans, are used as ingredients.

Preparation time: 10 minutes

Cooking time: 3 hours

Quantity: 20 portions

3-pound turkey ground • 1 ½ cup brown rice • 1 drained and washed can kidney beans (15 oz. / 420g) • 1 ½ cups peeled and sliced sweet potato • 1 ½ cups peeled and sliced carrots • 1 cup chopped green beans • ½ quarts (liters) water

1. In a large slow cooker, combine all of the ingredients and stir to combine with the water.

2. Cook on low for 6 hours or more.

Easy Slow Beef and Beans

This is a very easy Slow cooker recipe. You can prepare it the day before and have it ready the next day when you are busy. In addition, you can add 1 cup of rice if you prefer.

Preparation time: 15 minutes

Cooking time: 6 hours minutes

Quantity: 6 servings

2 1/2 lbs. (1100g) ground beef • 1 (15 oz./400g) can kidney beans, rinsed and drained • 1 1/2 cups butternut squash in small cubes • 1 1/2 cups carrots, finely chopped • 3/4 cup peas, fresh or frozen

1. In a large mixing basin, combine all of the ingredients. Place the mixture in a slow cooker.

2. Pour in 4 cups of water and cook on low for 6 hours.

Slow Chicken

A slow cooker is a wonderful way to save time because it's set and forget. Even while you sleep, the slow cooker blends the ingredients together into a delectable dinner. In the morning, your kitchen will smell incredible!

Preparation time: 10 minutes

Cooking time: 12 hours

Quantity: 9 cups

1 cup brown rice, uncooked • 3 chicken breasts, boneless and skinless • 2 carrots, peeled and cut into rounds • 1 cubed sweet potato (unpeeled but with any green parts removed) • ½ cup cranberries • water

1. Fill a 4-quart (4-liter) slow cooker halfway with water and add everything.

2. Cook for 12 hours or more on low.

Slow Beef and Turkey

This is a simple approach to add variety to your dog's diet. I make a big batch of food and divide it into smaller amounts before freezing it in various portions. The eggshells will offer calcium to your dog.

Preparation time: 20 minutes

Cooking time: 10 hours

Quantity: 9 cups

1 lb. (450g) ground beef • 1 lb. (450g) turkey ground • 2 carrots, big • 1 lb. (450g) of sweet potato • 1 potato • broccoli florets • cauliflower florets • 1 apple • 2 eggs • 1 tbsp flax seed, ground • 1 tbsp of parsley • 1 tsp turmeric powder • 1 tsp ginger powder • 1 tsp of cinnamon

1. Combine the beef and turkey in a slow cooker.

2. Using an electric hand mixer, fully mix the eggs, including the shells, until they are completely combined. The shells will break down into tiny fragments. Pour this mixture on over the meat.

3. Add the spices, fruit and vegetables to the slow cooker and mix.

4. Cook on low for 10 hours or more.

Slow Chicken and Potatoes

Make room in your meal rotation. This slow-cooker meal is sure to be a hit every time!

Preparation time: 20 minutes

Cooking time: 12 hours

Quantity: 8 servings

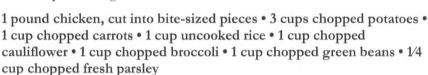

1 pound chicken, cut into bite-sized pieces • 3 cups chopped potatoes • 1 cup chopped carrots • 1 cup uncooked rice • 1 cup chopped cauliflower • 1 cup chopped broccoli • 1 cup chopped green beans • 1/4 cup chopped fresh parsley

1. Put the chicken, parsley, potatoes, carrots, and rice into the slow cooker. Add enough water to cover the ingredients completely and cook for 6 hours.

2. Add the cauliflower, broccoli, green beans and cook for another 6 hours.

Chickpea Stew

This nutrient-dense dish made with chickpeas, a canine superfood, is great for you and your dog to share. It's excellent served alongside couscous or rice.

Preparation time: 30 minutes

Cooking time: 6 hours

Quantity: 9 cups

1 tbsp extra-virgin olive oil • 1 cup carrot slices (¼"/0.6cm -thick) • 1 tsp brown sugar • 1 tsp peeled and grated fresh ginger • 3 cups cooked chickpeas • 1½ cups peeled and cubed baking potato • 1 cup diced green bell pepper • 1 cup cut green beans • 1 (14.5-ounce/410g) can diced tomatoes, undrained • 1¾ cups water or vegetable stock • 3 cups fresh baby spinach • 1 cup light coconut milk

1. In a large nonstick saucepan, sauté the carrot in oil for 5 minutes. Stir in brown sugar and ginger. Cook for 1 more minute, stirring constantly.

2. Place mixture in a slow cooker. Add chickpeas, potato, bell pepper, green beans, tomatoes, spinach and water or stock. Cook on high for 6 hours until the vegetables are tender.

3. Add coconut milk and allow to cool. Refrigerate for up to 3 days.

09

Meals & Pastries for Special Occasions

Holidays and celebrations are for everyone in the family, two-legged and four-legged alike! In this chapter, you'll find a variety of holiday recipes for your dog that include entire foods that you usually buy for traditional holiday dishes, such as turkey, cranberries, and pumpkin.

The key to properly enjoying this special cuisine, like with our personal holiday celebrations, is to never overindulge. It's crucial to enjoy the holidays and make happy memories with your dog by feeding him in moderation and keeping in mind his size, age, and activity level.

Bacon Pretzels

These delicious pretzels can be served as an appetizer. They're addictive, so be careful!

Preparation time: 40 minutes

Cooking time: 15 minutes

Quantity: 12 treats

1 packet active instant yeast (2 ¼ tbsp) • 1 ½ cup water • 1 tsp kosher salt • 1 tbsp sugar • 4 cups flour (all-purpose) • 1 lb. (450g) bacon strips

1. Preheat the oven to 425°F (220°C). A baking tray should be lightly oiled.

2. Dissolve yeast in warm water, stirring slowly. Add the salt and sugar when it has dissolved.1 cup at a time, add flour until dough is no longer sticky.

3. Roll out the dough on a floured surface. Knead the dough and divide it into 12 equal pieces. Using your hands, form each piece into a breadstick.

4. Wrap a strip of bacon around each breadstick, covering the entire treat.

5. Place on the baking tray, bake for 15 minutes until the bacon has crisped up.

Birthday Cupcake

Preparation time: 20 minutes

Cooking time: 30 minutes

Quantity: 4 cupcakes

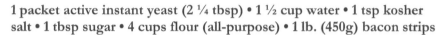

1 cup flour • 1 egg • ¼ cup peanut butter • ¼ cup pureed pumpkin • 1 tsp bicarbonate of soda • ¼ cup butter, melted • ½ cup of liquid *FROSTING:* ¼ lb. (110g) washed and cooked chicken liver • 4 oz. (110g) cream cheese, warmed to near-room temperature

1. Preheat the oven to 350°F (180°C) and grease a cupcake tin.

2. Combine all cupcake ingredients in a big mixing bowl until well mixed.

3. Fill cupcake tins halfway with the batter. Bake for 30 minutes.

4. Place the chicken liver in a medium mixing bowl to make the icing. Use a fork to crush it and combine it with the cream cheese.

5. Before serving add the frosting to the cupcakes.

Patties for St. Patrick's Day

For your beloved Irish Setters and Terriers at home! Peas are used in this dish to give the patties a green tint, and your dogs will adore the flavor.

Preparation time: 30 minutes

Cooking time: 25 minutes

Quantity: 30 treats

½ cup flour (all-purpose) • 1 cup flour (whole wheat) • 1 tbsp baking powder • 4 bacon slices, diced • 4 cups green peas • 3 tsp of water

1. Preheat the oven to 350°F (180°C). A baking tray should be lightly oiled.

2. Combine the dry ingredients. Cook bacon in a small skillet.

3. In a blender or food processor, purée the peas with the water. In a separate mixing dish, combine the peas and bacon; then mix in all of the dry ingredients.

4. Knead the dough on a lightly floured surface, pat out or roll to a thickness of less than 1-2 inches (2-5cm). Use cookie cutters to make designs.

5. Place them on the baking tray, bake for 25 minutes, or until golden brown.

Valentine's Day Red Bell Pepper Cookies

Preparation time: 30 minutes

Cooking time: 30 minutes

Quantity: 18 treats

1 red bell pepper (½ oz./15g) • ¼ cup chicken broth (homemade) • 2 eggs • 1 tbsp plain low-fat yogurt • 2 tbsp extra-virgin olive oil • 3 ½ cup rice flour • ½ cup cooked chicken, crumbled • 1 cup carrots, minced

1. Preheat the oven to 350°F (180°C). Prepare a baking tray.

2. Remove the red bell peppers stem, core, and seeds. Dice into small pieces.

3. In a large mixing bowl, combine flour, broth, eggs, yogurt, and olive oil. Toss in the chicken and vegetables. Combine thoroughly.

4. Using a spoon, scoop out golf ball-sized balls from the dough. Spread out and flatten with the back of a fork on a baking tray. Bake for 30 minutes.

Chicken Witches Fingers for Halloween

This version of the popular Witches' Fingers cookie replaces sugar with savory chicken, and the red gel with molasses. It will look like blood when it oozes out from beneath the almond nail. This is a healthy, protein-packed treat sure to become your furry friend's new favorite.

Preparation time: 40 minutes

Cooking time: 25 minutes

Quantity: 20 cookies

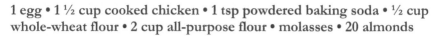

1 egg • 1 ½ cup cooked chicken • 1 tsp powdered baking soda • ½ cup whole-wheat flour • 2 cup all-purpose flour • molasses • 20 almonds

1. Preheat the oven to 350°F (180°C). Prepare a baking tray.

2. In a blender, purée the chicken until it resembles baby food, adding a little water if required. Stir in the egg and baking powder.

3. In a medium mixing basin, combine the flours. Combine with the chicken mixture, then knead the dough.

4. Take a golf ball-sized piece of dough and shape it into a 4" (10cm) long tube with your hands. Place it on the baking tray.

5. At the end fill a tiny hole with molasses. Place a single almond on top and gently press it down. The almond should be pointing outwards, like a fingernail.

6. Bake for 20–25 minutes.

Turkey and Cranberry Treats

Do you have any leftovers of turkey and cranberries that you're not sure what to do with? Make a tasty and nutritious treat for your dog with this recipe. This pleasant treat can be done with leftovers or prepare some turkey or chicken for it.

Preparation time: 40 minutes

Cooking time: 25 minutes

Quantity: 36 treats

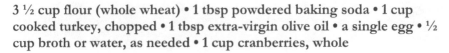

3 ½ cup flour (whole wheat) • 1 tbsp powdered baking soda • 1 cup cooked turkey, chopped • 1 tbsp extra-virgin olive oil • a single egg • ½ cup broth or water, as needed • 1 cup cranberries, whole

1. Preheat the oven to 350°F (180°C). Grease two baking trays lightly.

2. In a large mixing bowl, combine the flour and baking powder. In a blender or food processor, combine the turkey, olive oil, and egg. Add some water or broth if necessary. Add the cranberries and continue to mix until the turkey has a smooth, spreadable consistency.

3. To create a thick dough, combine the liquid with the dry ingredients in a mixing bowl and whisk.

4. Knead the dough on a lightly floured surface. Because this is a substantial dough, you'll need to use some force.

5. Cut the dough into cookie form and place on the baking trays. Bake for 25 minutes.

6. Allow to cool completely before serving or storing. Refrigerate for 3 days or freeze for up to 6 months in an airtight container.

Mini Pumpkin Muffins

If you don't have any homemade pumpkin purée on hand, you can make this simple dish with a can of pureed pumpkin. This is a healthy recipe that your furry friend will love.

Preparation time: 20 minutes

Cooking time: 20 minutes

Quantity: 36 treats

Rice flour (1 2/3 cup) • 1 tbsp baking soda • ¼ tsp of cinnamon • 2 tbsp molasses • 1 ¾ cup pureed pumpkin • ½ cup canola olive oil • 2 gently beaten eggs • water (⅓ cup)

1. Preheat the oven to 350°F (180°C). Grease a very small muffin tin or use parchment cups.

2. Combine rice flour, baking soda, cinnamon, and molasses in a large mixing basin, then add pumpkin purée, oil, and eggs. Add more water as needed until the mixture resembles mashed potatoes.

3. Fill muffin cups halfway with the mixture and bake for 20 minutes.

Thanksgiving Frittata

Are you having trouble figuring out what to do with your Thanksgiving leftovers? A frittata is a simple and hearty meal for both you and your dog.

Preparation time: 10 minutes

Cooking time: 25 minutes

Quantity: 6 servings

6 quail eggs • ½ cup pumpkin • 2 tbsp extra-virgin olive oil • ½ cup cooked green beans, chopped • 1 cup leftover turkey, chopped

1. In a mixing dish, combine the egg and pumpkin.

2. Over medium heat, warm the olive oil in a large pan and cook the turkey and green beans to your desired doneness.

3. Reduce the heat to a medium-low setting. Pour the egg mixture over the turkey and green beans. Cook for around 15 minutes until the sauce has thickened.

Brown Betty

Brown Betty is a traditional American meal. The Brown Betty is a cobbler-style dessert made with fruit (typically apples) and a bread crumb topping. This dish is completely safe for your dog to eat, but is not necessarily healthy. Make it as an occasional treat.

Preparation time: 30 minutes

Cooking time: 45 minutes

Quantity: 4 Cup

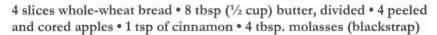

4 slices whole-wheat bread • 8 tbsp (½ cup) butter, divided • 4 peeled and cored apples • 1 tsp of cinnamon • 4 tbsp. molasses (blackstrap)

1. Preheat the oven to 350°F (180°C). Grease a pie pan or an 8" x 8" (20x20cm) baking dish with half of the butter.

2. Crumble the bread by hand or cut it into tiny pieces. Thinly slice the apples.

3. Overlap layers of bread and apples in the pie pan before sprinkling with cinnamon. Top with butter slices and drizzle with molasses.

4. Cover with aluminum foil, bake until golden brown, about 30-45 minutes.

Festive Pumpkin Cupcakes

Dog cupcakes are extremely popular these days, just like human cupcakes. These are delicious on their own, but they may be decorated with cream cheese icing to add a personal touch.

Preparation time: 10 minutes

Cooking time: 35 minutes

Quantity: 10 treats

a single egg • 1 tsp molasses • 1 tsp bicarbonate of soda • 1 cup flour (all-purpose) • 1 cup pureed pumpkin • ¼ cup butter, melted

1. Preheat the oven to 350°F (180°C).

2. Prepare a muffin tin by lightly greasing it.

3. Combine all ingredients in a medium mixing basin and thoroughly combine.

4. Bake for 30–35 minutes, until a toothpick inserted in the center of a cupcake comes out clean.

Christmas Fruitcake

If you're looking to give a special gift, look no further. This fruitcake will make a great impression on Santa when he makes his big night. Doggy adores fruitcakes, too!

Preparation time: 20 minutes

Cooking time: 30 minutes

Quantity: 16 treats

1 cup cranberries, fresh • 1 peeled and cored apple • 2 cups all-purpose flour • 1 cup pecans or almonds, divided • ⅓ cup molasses • a single egg • 1 tsp powdered baking soda • a pinch of cinnamon • 1 quart (liter) of water

1. Preheat the oven to 350°F (180°C). Spray muffin tins or use parchment cups.

2. Chop the cranberries, apple, and half of the almonds in a blender.

3. In a large mixing basin, combine all of the other ingredients. Whisk in the cranberry-apple-nut mixture after they've been combined.

4. Fill the muffin cups halfway with batter. The remaining nuts should be scattered on top. Bake for 30 minutes.

Easter Carrot Cookies

Preparation time: 30 minutes

Cooking time: 30 minutes

Quantity: 28 cookies

2 cups oats, rolled • 2 cups flour • 1 cup carrots, grated • 2 tbsp molasses • 2 large eggs • ½ cup butter • 2 tbsp powdered baking soda • FROSTING: 4 oz. (110g) cream cheese

1. Preheat the oven to 350°F (180°C). Prepare two baking trays.

2. Combine all of the ingredients with ½ cup of water and mix well.

3. On a lightly floured surface, roll out the dough to a thickness of ¼ inches (0,5cm). Cut out the dough into cookie shapes.

4. Bake for 30 minutes, or until golden brown. Allow the cookies to cool before sandwiching them with softened cream cheese between two cookies.

10

Homemade Kibble

If you have a busy life, making your own kibble can help take some of the pressure off. Also, if you're traveling and need to bring some meals for your dog, homemade kibble is a good option.

The most important thing is making sure you are using a good, high-quality ingredients as the base for your kibble. When buying commercial kibble, you will often find cheap and highly processed ingredients, including by-products and ingredients that can be harmful to your pet. With homemade kibble you will always know and understand what you are feeding your pet.

Kibble Variations

This kibble recipe is a template for variations. You can add beets, broccoli, brown rice, carrots, flaxseed meal, green beans, peas, potatoes, rolled oats, rosemary leaf, and more.

Preparation time: 40 minutes

Cooking time: 60 minutes

Quantity: 20 servings

2 cups rye flour • 4 cups whole wheat flour • 2 cups nonfat milk powder • 2 teaspoons bone meal • 1 cup plain wheat germ • 1/2 cup chopped fresh parsley • 4 eggs • 1 cup olive oil • 4 tablespoons Worcestershire sauce • 3 cups water • 4 cups cooked ground beef, lamb, chicken or turkey • 2 cups cooked and puréed sweet potatoes • 11/2 cups chopped dried apples • 2 cups frozen chopped spinach, thawed

1. Preheat the oven to 300°F (150°C). Prepare two large baking trays.

2. In a large mixing bowl, combine the flours, milk powder, bone meal, wheat germ, parsley, Worcestershire sauce, oil and water.

3. Fold in the egg and combine it all evenly. Add the meat, sweet potatoes, dried apples, and spinach and press them into the dough.

4. Spread the dough on the baking trays, making it very flat and thin. Use a knife to cut it into small squares.

5. Bake for 45 minutes to 1 hour until the kibble is golden brown. During the baking process, move the kibble around on the baking tray so that it bakes evenly.

6. It will be hot and moist when you take your kibble out of the oven. Let it rest on cooling racks for two hours, until it is completely dry and cold.

7. Refrigerate for up to 7 days or freeze for up to 6 months in an airtight container.

Beef Kibble

This is a delicious and simple recipe for homemade beef kibble that your dog will enjoy! It's very easy to make, and the end result is crunchy, delicious kibble.

Preparation time: 40 minutes

Cooking time: 60 minutes

Quantity: 20 servings

2 cups rye flour • 4 cups whole wheat flour • 2 cups nonfat milk powder • 2 teaspoons bone meal • 1/2 cup rolled oats • 2 teaspoons bone meal • 1 cup plain wheat germ • 1 teaspoon kosher salt • 1/2 cup chopped fresh parsley • 4 eggs • 1 cup olive oil • 4 tablespoons Worcestershire sauce • 3 cups water • 4 cups ground beef, cooked and then puréed • 2 cups cooked and puréed sweet potatoes • 2 cups frozen chopped spinach, thawed and drained

1. Preheat the oven to 300°F (150°C). Prepare two large baking trays.

2. In a large mixing bowl, combine the flours, milk powder, rolled oats, bone meal, wheat germ, parsley, Worcestershire sauce, oil and water.

3. Fold in the egg and combine it all evenly. Add the meat, sweet potatoes and spinach and press them into the dough.

4. Spread the dough on the baking trays, making it very flat and thin. Use a knife to cut it into small squares.

5. Bake for 45 minutes to 1 hour until the kibble is golden brown. During the baking process, move the kibble around on the baking tray so that it bakes evenly.

6. It will be hot and moist when you take your kibble out of the oven. Let it rest on cooling racks for two hours, until it is completely dry and cold.

7. Refrigerate for up to 7 days or freeze for up to 6 months in an airtight container.

Chicken and Sardines Kibble

Making your own kibble allows you to have complete control over your dog's nutrition while also being a cost-effective alternative to expensive commercial kibble.

Preparation time: 40 minutes

Cooking time: 90 minutes

Quantity: 3 lbs. (1300g) of kibble

1 ½ cup water, divided • 1 lb. (450g) chicken gizzards, cooked • 9 ½ cup whole-wheat flour • can sardines (3.75-ounce/100g) in water • 1 cup powdered nonfat dry milk • 2 eggs • ⅓ cup olive oil

1. Preheat the oven to 350°F (180°C). Prepare two baking trays.

2. Puree the sweet potatoes in a blender or food processor with ¾ cup water. Peeling and cutting the potatoes is recommended.

3. Place the gizzards in a blender or food processor and finely mince with ¾ cups water. Blend in the sardines until smooth.

4. In a large mixing basin, combine the flour, milk powder, eggs, and olive oil. Add the sweet potato purée, gizzards and sardines. Mix thoroughly.

5. Roll out the dough on a floured surface. Add additional flour as needed. Roll it out to a thickness of ¼ –½ inches (0.6-1.2cm).

6. Cut strips with a pizza cutter and place them on the baking trays. Space the strips at least ½" (1.2cm) apart.

7. Bake for 45 minutes before turning the strips. Cut strips into squares with a pizza cutter. You may personalize the size to your dog's liking. Return the baking trays to the oven for another 45 minutes of baking.

8. Let the kibble rest on cooling racks for two hours, until it is completely dry and cold.

9. Refrigerate for up to 7 days or freeze for up to 6 months.

Stomach friendly Kibble

Preparation time: 20 minutes

Cooking time: 45 minutes

Quantity: 12 cups

3 cups cooked rice • 3 cups rolled oats • 2 cups rice flour • 2 tbsp. bone meal • 3 cups homemade broth • 1 cup silken tofu, pureed • 1/2 cup olive oil

1. Mix the dry ingredients in a mixing cup and then add the broth.

2. Preheat the oven to 200°F (95°C).

3. Pat the mixture onto a baking tray with a thickness a thickness of ½ inches (1.2cm). Bake for 45 minutes.

4. Allow to cool slightly, and cut or break into small pieces.

5. Refrigerate for up to 7 days or freeze for up to 6 months.

Hearty Granola Bars

Preparation time: 15 minutes

Cooking time: 45 minutes

Quantity: 6 cups

2 cups of flour • 1 cup of rolled oats • 1 cup of wheat germ • ½ cup of cooked quinoa • 1 egg • 1½ cup of homemade chicken broth

1. Combine all of the ingredients in a large mixing bowl until completely combined. Let it sit for roughly 20 minutes to half an hour before rolling it out.

2. Preheat the oven to 325°F (160°C). Prepare a baking tray.

3. Place the mixture onto a surface and start rolling it out. Roll it out to a thickness of ½ inches (1.2cm). It's up to you how big or little you cut the treat into. Depending on your dog's preference, cut them into bars or smaller pieces.

4. Place them onto the baking tray and bake for about 45 minutes.

5. Let the bars rest on cooling racks for two hours.

Pumpkin Chicken Kibble

Pumpkin is loaded with fiber, is low in calories, and has lots of beta carotene and vitamin A. It's also naturally sweet, which dogs love.

Preparation time: 40 minutes

Cooking time: 60 minutes

Quantity: 20 servings

2 cups rye flour • 4 cups whole wheat flour • 2 cups nonfat milk powder • 1⁄2 cup rolled oats • 2 teaspoons bone meal • 1 cup plain wheat germ • 1⁄2 cup chopped fresh parsley • 4 eggs • 1 cup olive oil • 1 cup molasses • 4 tablespoons Worcestershire sauce • 3 cups water • 4 cups ground chicken, cooked and then puréed • 2 cups canned pumpkin • 2 cups frozen chopped spinach, thawed • 1 cup dried apples, crushed • 11⁄2 cups dried veggies (mixture)

1. Preheat the oven to 300°F (150°C). Prepare two large baking trays.

2. In a large mixing bowl, combine the flours, rolled oats, milk powder, bone meal, wheat germ, parsley, Worcestershire sauce, molasses, oil and water.

3. Add the egg and mix it in evenly. Add the chicken, pumpkins, dried apples, dried veggies and spinach and press them into the dough.

4. Spread the dough on the baking trays, making it very flat and thin. Use a knife to cut it into small squares.

5. Bake for 45 minutes to 1 hour until the kibble is golden brown. During the baking process, move the kibble around on the baking tray so that it bakes evenly.

6. It will be hot and moist when you take your kibble out of the oven. Let it rest on cooling racks for two hours, until it is completely dry and cold.

7. Refrigerate for up to 7 days or freeze for up to 6 months in an airtight container.

Turkey Knuckles

Despite the fact that most DIY diets do not contain kibble as the first component, this is a good recipe to have on hand. It's a convenient treat that your dog will love.

Preparation time: 50 minutes

Cooking time: 90 minutes

Quantity: 20

8 ½ cup flour (whole wheat) • 2 cups powdered nonfat dry milk • 2 eggs • ½ cup extra-virgin olive oil • 1 lb. (450g) lean ground turkey, uncooked • a cup of puréed, skinless cooked sweet potato (or substitute pumpkin, green beans, or a mix)

1. Preheat the oven to 350°F (180°C). Prepare a baking tray.

2. Combine flour, dry milk powder, eggs, and olive oil in a large mixing basin. Combine the ground turkey and vegetable purée in a mixing bowl. Mix thoroughly.

3. Roll out the dough to a thickness of ¼ –½ inches (0.6-1.2cm) on a lightly floured surface.

4. Cut strips with a pizza cutter and place them on the baking trays. Space the strips at least ½" (1.2cm) apart.

5. Bake for 45 minutes before turning the strips. Cut strips into squares with a pizza cutter. You may personalize the size to your dog's liking. Return the baking trays to the oven for another 45 minutes of baking.

6. Let the kibble rest on cooling racks for two hours, until it is completely dry and cold.

7. Refrigerate for up to 7 days or freeze for up to 6 months.

11

Side Dishes

Do you want to make a delicious and healthy side dish? While we've included a variety of well-rounded one-dish meals, it's also nice to cook and serve a tasty side dish with your meaty main dish.

If you want an easy way to add a side dish, seasonal fruits and vegetables can always be transformed into sides and added to your dog's favorite meat dinner.

Pumpkin Purée

Puréed pumpkin is an excellent addition to many dogs treat and meal recipes. Canned pumpkin may be used, but only if it is unsweetened.

Preparation time: 20 minutes

Cooking time: 40 minutes

Quantity: 2-4 cups

1 small cooking pumpkin • Water, as needed

1. Preheat the oven to 350°F (180°C). Prepare a baking tray.

2. Cut the top off of the pumpkin after washing it and cut it into quarters.

3. Use a spoon to remove seeds. You can keep the seeds to make pepitas.

4. Place the pumpkin quarters on the baking tray and bake for 30–40 minutes.

5. Allow to cool. Remove pumpkin skin and chop the pumpkin flesh into cubes. Add cubes to a blender with enough water to make a purée that resembles baby food.

6. Freeze purée in 1-cup containers or ice cube trays.

Pepitas

Don't forget to save the pumpkin seeds! Protein, amino acids, fiber, iron, copper, phosphorus, magnesium, calcium, zinc, potassium, folic acid, and niacin are all found in them.

Preparation time: 10 minutes

Cooking time: 20-30 minutes

Quantity: ½ –2 cups, depending on pumpkin size

Seeds of 1 pumpkin • 1 tbsp olive oil

1. Remove and discard the pulp from the seeds. Spread out the seeds on a baking tray overnight to dry.

2. Preheat the oven to 350°F (180°C).

3. Combine seeds and olive oil on baking tray,. Season with dog-friendly spices.

4. Bake for 20-30 minutes. Allow to cool completely before serving.

Loaves of Lentil

Lentils are a high-protein, low-calorie food for dogs who are on a weight loss plan. Lentils are also a source of several vitamins and minerals.

Preparation time: 20 minutes

Cooking time: 25 minutes

Quantity: 8 muffins

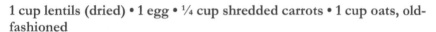

1 cup lentils (dried) • 1 egg • ¼ cup shredded carrots • 1 cup oats, old-fashioned

1. Preheat the oven to 350°F (180°C). Grease or line a muffin tray with parchment paper cups.

2. Cook lentils until tender according per package directions. Remove the pan from the heat and drain the water. Fill a medium bowl halfway with lentils.

3. To mash lentils, use a fork or a potato masher. Stir in the carrots, egg, and oats once the mixture has cooled.

4. Fill muffin cups 2/3 full with the mixture and bake for 25 minutes.

5. Allow to cool before serving. Refrigerate for up to 5 days or freeze for up to 6 months in an airtight container.

Supplement Veggies

Seasonal buying allows you to take advantage of discounts and freshness while also allowing you to test new greens. To match the produce available, you may alter the veggies in this dish.

Preparation time: 10 minutes

Cooking time: 5 minutes

Quantity: 4-5 cups

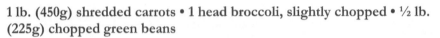

1 lb. (450g) shredded carrots • 1 head broccoli, slightly chopped • ½ lb. (225g) chopped green beans

1. Peel and chop all vegetables. In a large mixing bowl, combine all of the vegetables, cover, and refrigerate.

2. Portion out the meal's serving, add 1 tbsp of water, and microwave for 3 minutes to add to your dog's dish.

Sweet Potato Pot stickers

Pot stickers are both nutritious and delicious. They're also suitable for you and your dog to consume. Wonton wrappers can be found in Asian markets.

Preparation time: 30 minutes

Cooking time: 20 minutes

Quantity: 12 pot stickers

1 cup sweet potato, cooked (roughly 2 medium sweet potatoes, peeled) • 1 tbsp fresh rosemary • ⅓ cup of ricotta cheese • 1 pack of wonton wrappers • ¼ cup grated Parmesan cheese • 1 tsp sunflower seed oil

1. Preheat the oven to 350°F (180°C).

2. In a blender or food processor, combine the sweet potato, rosemary, and cheeses. Pulse until well combined.

3. Add 1 tbsp of the sweet potato and cheese stuffing should be placed in the middle of a wonton wrapper; seal the edges with oil to keep them closed.

4Place the wontons on a baking tray and coat with sunflower oil.

5. Bake for 15–20 minutes until golden brown.

Kiwi and Canine Kale

Serve this side dish with your dog's favorite meat dish for a nutritious and delicious meal. Kiwi fruit is high in fiber, potassium, and vitamin C. Kale is a nutritious vegetable for both dogs and people.

Preparation time: 5 minutes

Cooking time: 10 minutes

Quantity: 3 cups

1 tbsp coconut oil • 1 tsp fresh ginger, peeled and minced • 1 tbsp oregano leaves, fresh • 2 peeled and sliced kiwis • 1 bunch of kale, washed and thinly sliced

1. Thinly slice the kale leaves. Peel and slice the Kiwi, then mince the ginger.

2. In a large skillet, cook the ginger in coconut oil for three minutes over medium-high heat. Add the oregano and kiwi and continue for 2 minutes.

3. Reduce the heat to low and add the kale; simmer for 5 minutes until soft.

Raw Vegetable Cupcakes

This is a meal made with fresh vegetables that can be served to your dog or easily frozen for later use. You can substitute the vegetables in this recipe with other options like asparagus, broccoli, cauliflower, collards, cabbage, cucumbers, squash, sweet potatoes and zucchini.

Preparation time: 15 minutes

Quantity: 30-50 treats

1 celery head, trimmed • 1 pack of carrots • 1/3 cup parsley • 1 Romaine lettuce or mustard greens

1. Wash and trim the vegetables.

2. Chop into squares and put 1 cup at a time to a food processor or blender to purée, adding water as needed.

3. Once all of the vegetables have been puréed freeze in ice cube trays or cupcake trays. Transfer to a zip-top plastic bag and store in the freezer.

4. Can be served as a frozen treat or thaw to room temperature before serving.

12

Sweet Treats

Do you have a dog that enjoys sweets? Although chocolate is harmful to dogs, you may offer your furry friend with a wide range of other rewards.

Many of these recipes include blackstrap molasses, which is high in nutrients and used as a sweetener, while others use fruits for taste. You'll be able to make tasty sweets with a touch of pear, pumpkin, blueberries, and other fruits.

Peanut Butter Biscuits

Peanut butter is a popular taste among dogs, including ours. If your dog can tolerate wheat, you may use whole wheat flour or all-purpose flour instead of chickpea flour in this easy recipe.

Preparation time: 40 minutes
Cooking time: 25 minutes
Quantity: 36 treats

1 mashed medium banana • 3 tbsp. organic creamy peanut butter (unsweetened) • 1 egg • 1 ¾ cup chickpea flour

1. Preheat the oven to 350°F (180°C). Line a baking tray with parchment paper

2. In a mixing basin, combine the banana, peanut butter, egg, and flour. Roll out the dough on a floured surface to a thickness of ¼ inches (0.6cm).

3. Cut the dough into 24 cookies with a cookie cutter or a pizza cutter. Place the cookies on a baking tray and bake for 25 minutes, or until golden brown.

Paleo Coconut and Carrots Treat

This Paleo dish is completely grain-free thanks to the use of coconut flour. Coconut is high in potassium and many other vitamins and minerals, as well as being tasty to dogs.

Preparation time: 20 minutes
Cooking time: 40 minutes
Quantity: 36 treats

½ pound (225g) carrots • ¼ cup of coconut chips • 2 eggs • ¼ cup of coconut flour

1. Preheat the oven to 350°F (180°C). Line a baking tray with parchment paper.

2. In a blender, combine the carrots and coconut chips until finely chopped.

3. Combine the carrot–coconut chip combination, eggs, and flour in a medium mixing basin. Stir until everything is thoroughly combined.

4. Using a fork, lightly flatten 1 tbsp of dough on the baking tray. Continue to add the batter until it has been used up.

5. Bake cookies for 40 minutes until golden brown.

Peanut Butter Chia Treats

Combining the antioxidants, calcium, and omega-3 fatty acids in chia seeds with the delectableness of peanut butter produces a specialty that your pup will be sure to love.

Preparation time: 30 minutes

Cooking time: 15 minutes

Quantity: 36 treats

½ cup oats, rolled • 1 tsp powdered baking soda • 1 tsp chia seeds • ½ cup flour (all-purpose or wheat) • ¾ cup unsweetened organic peanut butter • 2 eggs • 1 tbsp molasses (blackstrap) • ¼ cup of coconut oil

1. Preheat the oven to 350°F (180°C). Prepare a baking tray.

2. Mix the oats, baking powder, chia seeds, and flour.

3. In a mixer, combine peanut butter, eggs, molasses, and coconut oil. Gradually add the dry mix to the wet mixture and combine

4. Put 1 tbsp of dough on the baking tray. Repeat until the batter is used up.

5. Bake for 10–15 minutes until golden brown.

Blueberry Fruit Strips

Blueberries are used to make this treat, but you may substitute with other fruit in season. The rolls are simple to break into little pieces for ideal snacks on long walks. If you have one, go with the food dehydrator instead of the oven.

Preparation time: 10 minutes

Cooking time: 7 hours

Quantity: 36 treats

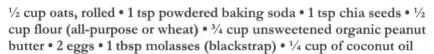

1 lb. (450g) blueberries • ¼ cup of lemon juice • 1 tbsp honey (raw)

1. Preheat the oven to 200°F (95°C). Using parchment paper, line a baking tray.

2. Purée all of the ingredients in a blender. If required, add a tbsp of water.

3. Spread the mixture evenly over the parchment paper.

4. Bake the rollups for 6–7 hours until they are no longer sticky. Remove from the oven and set aside to cool completely. Refrigerate after cutting into strips.

Granola Bars

Regular granola bars are not suitable for dogs since they include too much sugar and sometimes even chocolate. The sweetness in these basic bars comes from better sources.

Preparation time: 15 minutes

Cooking time: 30 minutes

Quantity: 36 treats

3 ½ cup oats, old fashioned • ¼ tsp of cinnamon • 1 tbsp molasses (blackstrap) • 1 cup unsweetened organic peanut butter • 1 cup of water ½ cup pumpkin preparation • ¼ cup of applesauce • ¼ cup of honey • ¼ cup coarsely chopped dry roasted peanuts

1. Preheat the oven to 350°F (180°C). Lightly grease an 8" x 8" (20x20cm) pan.

2. Combine all of the ingredients in a large mixing basin.

3. After filling the mixture into the prepared pan, bake for 30 minutes.

4. Chill for at least 4 hours to solidify and cut into squares.

Pumpkin and Peanut Butter Treats

You might give one to your dog and try one yourself!

Preparation time: 20 minutes

Cooking time: 20 minutes

Quantity: 30 treats

2 ½ cup flour (whole wheat) • ½ cup pureed pumpkin • ½ cup unsweetened organic peanut butter • 2 tsp cinnamon powder • 1 tsp powdered baking soda • ½ cup water, if necessary

1. Preheat the oven to 350°F (180°C). Grease two baking trays.

2. Mix all ingredients except the water in a medium bowl. Pour in the water until the mixture reaches a good consistency. Depending on the type of peanut butter, the amount of water might vary.

3. Knead the dough on a floured surface and roll it out to a thickness of ¼ inches (0.6cm). Cut the dough into 30 pieces and arrange on the baking trays.

4. Bake in the oven for 20 minutes.

Cranberry Dog Treats

Cranberry is high in vitamin C, fiber, manganese, antioxidants, and has traditionally been used to treat urinary tract infections.

Preparation time: 45 minutes

Cooking time: 30 minutes

Quantity: 40 treats

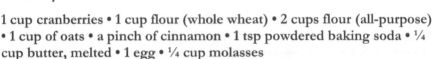

1 cup cranberries • 1 cup flour (whole wheat) • 2 cups flour (all-purpose) • 1 cup of oats • a pinch of cinnamon • 1 tsp powdered baking soda • ¼ cup butter, melted • 1 egg • ¼ cup molasses

1. Preheat the oven to 350°F (180°C). Grease two baking trays.

2. In a food processor, chop the cranberries. Mix the flours, oats, cinnamon, and baking powder. Next, add the melted butter, chopped cranberries, egg, and molasses. Gradually pour in the water until everything is completely mixed.

3. Knead the dough on a lightly floured surface and roll it out to a thickness of ¼ inches (0.6cm). Cut the dough into 40 different shapes with cookie cutters.

4. Bake for 30 minutes after placing the treats on the baking trays.

Peanut Butter and Banana Dog Treats

Penny enjoyed this so many times, I could make it with my eyes closed.

Preparation time: 10 minutes

Cooking time: 3 minutes

Quantity: 1

2 tbsp. eanut butter or other nut butter • 2 wheat bread slices • mashed ripe banana • bacon grease, butter, or frying oil

1. Sandwich the peanut butter and the mashed banana between the bread.

2. In a large skillet, sauté the sandwich in the grease over low heat for 3 minutes on each side until golden brown.

3. Allow to cool before cutting into little pieces with a knife or cookie cutters. Don't attempt to slice it while it's still warm; the peanut butter will ooze out!

Peanut Butter Bones

Preparation time: 20 minutes
Cooking time: 30 minutes
Quantity: 24 treats

1 cup whole wheat flour • 1 cup all-purpose flour • 2 tsp baking powder
• 1 cup multigrain cereal flakes, crushed • ½ cup carrots, shredded • 2
tbsp olive oil • 1 tbsp molasses • 1 cup peanut butter • ½ cup of water

1. Preheat the oven to 350°F (180°C). Line a baking tray with parchment paper.

2. In a large mixing bowl, combine the dry ingredients, then add the carrots, olive oil, molasses and peanut butter.

3. Pour in the water until the mixture reaches a good consistency. Depending on the type of peanut butter, the amount of water might vary. Knead the dough.

4. Roll out the dough on a floured surface to a thickness of ¼ inches (0.6cm). Using a knife, cut the dough into 24 bone shapes.

5. Arrange the cookies on a baking tray and bake for 30 minutes.

Grain-Free Treats

Preparation time: 40 minutes
Cooking time: 45 minutes
Quantity: 36 treats

2 tsp of water • 1 ½ tablespoons flaxseed, ground • 1 peeled, boiled, and
mashed sweet potato • 1 egg • ¼ cup of coconut milk • ½ cup
unsweetened organic peanut butter • ½ cup cultured coconut flour

1. Preheat the oven to 350°F (180°C). Line a baking tray with parchment paper.

2. Mix sweet potato, egg, coconut milk, peanut butter, and coconut flour.

3. In a small dish, mix the flaxseed with a spoonful of water. Stir in the mix.

4. Place 1 tbsp of dough on a baking tray. Repeat until the batter is gone.

5. Bake for 40–45 minutes until golden brown.

Pear and Molasses Dog Biscuits

Pear seeds (or apple seeds, for that matter) should not be fed to your dog. Pear flesh, on the other hand, is a nutritious and healthy treat that I love giving my dogs. Pears are high in water-soluble fiber and vitamin C.

Preparation time: 20 minutes

Cooking time: 30 minutes

Quantity: 1

2 ½ cup whole-wheat flour • 2 cups cored and diced pears • 1 cup of water • 1 tbsp powdered baking soda • 3 tbsp molasses

1. Preheat the oven to 350°F (180°C). Prepare a baking tray.

2. In a large mixing basin, combine the ingredients to create a thick, sticky dough. Knead the dough and roll it out to a thickness of ¼ inches (0.6cm).

3. Make 16 squares from the dough. Arrange the biscuits on a baking tray.

4. Bake for 30 minutes until the bottoms of the biscuits are golden brown.

Peanut Butter and Applesauce Dog Biscuits

Preparation time: 20-40 minutes

Cooking time: 25 minutes

Quantity: 36 treats

3 cups flour (whole wheat) • 2 cups oats • 1 cup unsweetened organic peanut butter • 1 cup applesauce, unsweetened • 1 tsp powdered baking soda

1. Preheat the oven to 350°F (180°C). Prepare two baking trays.

2. In a large mixing basin, combine all of the ingredients and stir until they are thoroughly combined and ready to knead. Knead the dough on a lightly floured surface. If the mixture is too crumbly, add a teaspoon of olive oil-

3. Roll out the dough to a thickness of ¼ inches (0.6cm), then cut it into 36 unique shapes. Place them on baking trays.

4. Bake for 25 minutes, or until gently browned.

Banana and Sunflower Dog Cookies

Combining banana and sunflower seed makes a wholesome treat that's as healthy as it is delicious. They are packed with vitamins and minerals.

Preparation time: 20 minutes

Cooking time: 20 minutes

Quantity: 24 treats

2 mashed ripe bananas • ½ cup olive oil • 2–2 ½ cup flour (all-purpose) • 1 cup sunflower seeds, shelled and unsalted • 1 tbsp powdered baking soda

1. Combine all of the ingredients in a large mixing bowl and mix until completely combined. Add additional flour to the recipe if it's too wet.

2. Place the bowl in the fridge for at least 30 minutes.

3. Preheat the oven to 350°F (180°C). Prepare a baking tray.

4. Make 24 small balls out of the dough. Place them on the baking tray and press down with a fork.

5. Bake for 15 minutes until golden brown.

Vegan Banana Cupcakes

Preparation time: 10 minutes

Cooking time: 15 minutes

Quantity: 24 treats

2 mashed ripe bananas • 2 tbsp agave nectar • ⅓ cup applesauce, unsweetened • 3 cups flour (whole wheat) • 1 ½ –2 tablespoons baking powder (organic) • 2 cups water

1. Preheat the oven to 350°F (180°C). Prepare small cupcake tins.

2. In a large mixing basin, mix bananas, agave nectar, and applesauce. Stir in the flour and baking powder gradually, then add the water little by little.

3. Fill two-thirds of the cupcake tins with batter. Bake for 15 minutes until a toothpick inserted in the center comes out clean.

Dog Treats to Counter Bad Breath

*Parsley is a natural breath freshener that might help your dog avoid having doggie breath.
Parsley-based diets assist keep your dog's teeth clean since some canines despise tooth brushing.*

Preparation time: 20 minutes

Cooking time: 30 minutes

Quantity: 24 treats

2 cups flour (whole wheat) • 1 cup oats, rolled • ½ cup powdered nonfat dry milk • 2 tbsp. fresh parsley, chopped • 2 eggs • 1 cup unsweetened organic peanut butter • ½ cup of liquid

1. Preheat the oven to 350°F (180°C). Prepare a baking tray.

2. Combine the flour, oats, nonfat dry milk powder, and parsley in a large mixing bowl. In a mixing cup, whisk together the eggs and then add the peanut butter and water.

3. Knead the dough on a floured surface and roll it to a thickness of 1 inch (2cm). Using cookie cutters, cut out 24 shapes. Bake for 30 minutes.

Anise Dog Treats

Preparation time: 20 minutes

Cooking time: 15 minutes

Quantity: 20 treats

2 cups flour (all-purpose) • 4 tbsp (¼ cup) softened butter • ¼ cup molasses • 1 egg • 2 tbsp anise seeds • 1 tsp powdered baking soda

1. Preheat the oven to 350°F (180°C). Two baking trays should be greased.

2. In a large mixing basin, combine all of the ingredients and stir them together until they are completely combined. The result is a dough that's rather sticky.

3. Pinch small bits the size of a large marble and roll between your palms before laying on the baking trays. Slightly flatten with a fork.

4. Bake for 15 minutes until golden brown.

Pumpkin Gingersnaps

Preparation time: 20 minutes

Cooking time: 15 minutes

Quantity: 36 treats

2 ½ cup flour (all-purpose) • 1 ½ tsp baking soda • 4 tbsp room temperature butter • 1 egg • 4 tbsp fresh ginger, peeled and finely grated • ½ cup pumpkin

1. Preheat the oven to 350°F (180°C). Prepare a baking tray.

2. In a medium mixing basin, combine flour and baking soda. Then add the butter, egg, ginger, and pumpkin. Make a thorough mixture.

3. Knead the dough on a floured surface until it is completely combined. Roll out the dough to a thickness of 1 inch (2cm) and use cookie cutters to cut out 36 shapes. Roll out the dough to an inch (1cm) if you want a chewier treat.

4. Bake for 15 minutes until golden brown.

Pumpkin Drops

This simple dish is ideal for senior dogs and those who are allergic to wheat.

Preparation time: 15 minutes

Cooking time: 20 minutes

Quantity: 24 treats

2 cups pureed pumpkin • ⅓ cup of cream of rice cereal • ½ cup powdered nonfat dry milk

1. Preheat the oven to 350°F (180°C). Line a baking tray with parchment paper or grease it.

2. Combine all ingredients in a large mixing bowl.

3. Place 1 tbsp of dough on a baking tray with a spoon. Repeat until the batter is gone. If desired, flatten slightly or leave as little balls.

4. Bake for 20 minutes until golden brown.

13

Savory Treats

Some dogs are more interested in tasty goods than sweet ones. Max loves anything with a beef taste, and the more pungent, the better. If your dog likes savory food, tiny bites of meals can be used as treats, either by itself or inside a toy.

Liver Cornbread

If you're hesitant about handling liver in dough, this dish will keep your hands off the liver.

Preparation time: 20 minutes

Cooking time: 30 minutes

Quantity: 48 treats

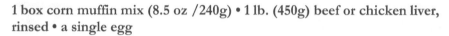

1 box corn muffin mix (8.5 oz /240g) • 1 lb. (450g) beef or chicken liver, rinsed • a single egg

1. Preheat the oven to 350°F (180°C). Prepare a baking tray with a 1-2" (3-5cm) edge.

2. Purée the liver in a blender. Combine the corn muffin mix and egg in a mixing basin, then add the liver.

3. Carefully pour the batter onto the prepared baking tray. Bake for 30 minutes.

4. Refrigerate after cooling before slicing. Refrigerate for up to 3 days or freeze for up to 6 months in an airtight container.

Cheeseburger Mini Treats

These meaty, cheesy, and delicious selections are sure to charm any dog. Instead of ground beef, you may use ground turkey in this delectable dish.

Preparation time: 30 minutes

Cooking time: 30 minutes

Quantity: 24 biscuits

1 lb. (450g) lean ground beef • ½ cup Cheddar cheese, shredded • 1 egg • smashed slices of toasted whole-wheat sandwich bread

1. Preheat the oven to 350°F (180°C). Prepare Mini-cupcake tins.

2. Combine the ingredients in a large mixing basin by hand and knead until the bread is evenly distributed.

3. Pinch off 1" (2.5cm) balls of the mixture and press into the cupcake tin.

4. Bake for 30 minutes until golden brown.

Surprise Pigskin Stuffing

This simple mixture can be stuffed into your dog's favorite treat-dispensing toy. It's sure to become your dog's favorite! You can substitute the cream cheese with peanut butter or soft bread.

Preparation time: 10 minutes
Quantity: 1 large container filled.

1 oz. (30g) cream cheese • 1 cup chicharrons or pig rinds, plain • 1 egg

1. Fill the small end of a clean container or a treat-dispensing toy with a little bit of the cream cheese.

2. In a mixing dish, combine chicharrons or pork rinds with a raw egg and crack the rinds just enough to allow the egg to soak in. If you're worried about raw eggs, cook them until they're semi-firm and then let them cool before serving.

3. Fill the toy with the mixture until it is completely filled. The remainder of the cream cheese should be filled into the larger opening of the toy.

Turkey Deli Rollups

This low-sodium turkey dish is perfect for you and your dog to share. It only takes a few minutes to make them. Because they aren't preserved, these homemade goodies have a short shelf life.

Preparation time: 5 minutes
Quantity: 30 treats

2 oz.(50g) cream cheese • ¼ lb. (110g) low-sodium turkey breast, sliced

1. Spread 1–2 teaspoons of cream cheese on a slice of turkey breast.

2. Roll tightly before slicing into 1" (2.5cm) pieces.

3. Refrigerate for up to 3 days, flattening the snacks to prevent them from unrolling.

Chicken and Cheese Biscuits

Consider using goat cheese in these savory biscuits if your dog is lactose intolerant; many dogs that are lactose intolerant may still stomach goat cheese. In addition, goat's milk cheese has a higher calcium content than cow's milk cheese, which promotes bone density.

Preparation time: 40 minutes

Cooking time: 30 minutes

Quantity: 24 biscuits

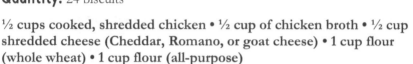

½ cups cooked, shredded chicken • ½ cup of chicken broth • ½ cup shredded cheese (Cheddar, Romano, or goat cheese) • 1 cup flour (whole wheat) • 1 cup flour (all-purpose)

1. Preheat the oven to 350°F (180°C). Line two baking trays with parchment paper or grease them.

2. In a blender or food processor, combine the turkey or chicken and half of the chicken stock until smooth.

3. In a large mixing bowl, combine the cheese and flours with the pureed mixture. Stir in a spoonful of the remaining liquid very gradually until the dough is workable.

4. Knead the dough on a floured surface and roll it out to a thickness of approximately ¼ inches (0.6cm). Cut out 24 shapes with cookie cutters.

5. Place the shapes on baking trays and bake for about 30 minutes.

6. Before serving or storing the biscuits, make sure they are absolutely cool.

Turkey Dog Biscuits with Oatmeal

Keep this dish in mind when creating treats for your furry friend. These easy-to-make biscuits will be wonderful with turkey. Chicken will work in a pinch if you don't have turkey.

Preparation time: 20 minutes

Cooking time: 25 minutes

Quantity: 24 biscuits

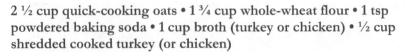

2 ½ cup quick-cooking oats • 1 ¾ cup whole-wheat flour • 1 tsp powdered baking soda • 1 cup broth (turkey or chicken) • ½ cup shredded cooked turkey (or chicken)

1. Preheat the oven to 350°F (180°C). Prepare two baking trays.

2. In a large mixing bowl, combine the dry ingredients. In a blender, combine the turkey and liquid and puree until smooth. Mix the meat and dry ingredients.

3. On a lightly floured surface, knead the dough. Cut the dough into shapes.

4. Put shapes on the baking trays. Bake for 25 minutes until golden brown.

Liver Logs

Dogs may munch on a nutritious chew with these stuffed celery stalks, which makes them a healthy chew alternative to rawhides and other chew sticks.

Preparation time: 20 minutes

Cooking time: 10 minutes

Quantity: 10-15 treats

Cream cheese, 8 oz. (220g) • 2 tablespoons olive oil • ½ lb. (220g) chicken liver, washed • 1 celery head

1. Remove the cream cheese from the refrigerator and let it soften.

2. In a large skillet, cook the liver over medium-high heat until it is well done. Remove the liver from the heat, then split it as much as possible with a fork.

3. Combine cream cheese and chicken livers. Stir until the liver is smooth.

4. Each treat consists of one celery stalk (no need to trim off the leaves). Fill with cream cheese–liver mixture by forking it in.

Chicken Liver Biscuits

Liver adds great taste to dog treats but it shouldn't be used for more than 5% of a dog's diet. The liver of a pig is particularly rich in vitamin A, which is why it's so highly utilized in dog treats. However, you can overfeed your dog with vitamin A if used too often.

Preparation time: 20 minutes

Cooking time: 30 minutes

Quantity: 35 treats

1 lb. (450g) washed chicken liver • 5 cups whole-wheat flour • 14.5-ounce (400g) can green beans, no salt added, drained • 1 egg • 1 cup brown rice flour

1. Preheat the oven to 350°F (180°C). Prepare two baking trays.

2. Add the chicken livers and green beans to a food processor or blender and puree. Continue to purée the mixture until it is almost completely smooth.

3. Combine the flour and egg, add the chicken liver and green bean combination to the mix. combine Until you've achieved a thick dough.

4. Roll out dough to a thickness of ½" (1.2cm) and cut with cookie cutters.

5. Bake for 30 minutes, checking for browning on the bottoms.

Liver Cupcakes

Preparation time: 20 minutes

Cooking time: 25 minutes

Quantity: 36 treats

1-pound cleaned chicken liver • 3 eggs • ¼ cup butter • 2 cups pureed pumpkin • 3 cups flour de coco • 1 tsp powdered baking soda

1. Preheat the oven to 350°F (180°C). Prepare small cupcake tins.

2. In a blender, puree the chicken liver. Once the liver has been pureed, add the eggs, butter, and pumpkin. Pulse to combine everything.

3. In a large mixing basin, combine the purée, flour, and baking powder.

4. Bake for 25 minutes after filling muffin pans 2/3 full.

Chopped Liver Stuffing

Preparation time: 40 minutes

Cooking time: 40 minutes

Quantity: Approximately 1 pound of filling

1 gallon (3.8l) of water • 1 lb. (450g) washed chicken liver • 2–3 finely sliced hardboiled eggs • (optional) vegetables

1. Bring a large pot of water to a boil and add the chicken livers. Cook for 40 minutes, reducing the heat if necessary.

2. Drain the liver and save the liquid; it's fantastic frozen in ice cube trays as a tasty treat!

3. With a fork or a potato masher, mash the livers and add the sliced eggs. Mix thoroughly.

4. Fill a pea-size amount of the mixture into a stuffing toy. Fill with a variety of your dog's favorite vegetables inside, such as green beans, celery, spinach, sweet potatoes, peas, and more. Close off with a spoonful of the stuffing.

Tuna Crackers

Preparation time: 15 minutes

Cooking time: 20 minutes

Quantity: 40 treats

1 cup cornmeal • 1 can (5-ounce/140g) chunked light or white tuna packed in water, not drained • 1 cup flour (all-purpose) • ⅓ cup water

1. Preheat the oven to 350°F (180°C). Line a baking tray with parchment paper or grease it.

2. Combine all ingredients by hand. Knead the dough on a floured surface and roll it out to a thickness of ¼ inches (0.6cm).

3. Using a pizza cutter, cut the dough into 40 crackers.

4. Place the crackers on a baking tray and bake for 20 minutes.

Sardine Stuffing

You may not picture sardines as a dog food if you think of them as such, but dogs can benefit from this nutrient-dense fish. Sardines are high in omega-3 fatty acids, vitamin D, and phosphorus, making them a healthy addition to treats.

Preparation time: 5 minutes
Quantity: 2 medium toys filled

1 sardine can (3.75 oz./100g) in water (do not drain) • ½ cup of cotton cheese • ½ cup Greek yogurt, plain

1. Combine all ingredients in a blender and blend until smooth.

2. Serve as a delicious garnish for a large meal or as stuffing for a container.

Carrots and Cheese Biscuits

Carrots are not only for rabbits; they're also a nutritious dog food, including meals, snacks, and raw. Carrots are a good source of fiber, low in calories, and high in beta carotene.

Preparation time: 25 minutes
Cooking time: 25 minutes
Quantity: 24 biscuits

1 cup carrots, shredded • 1 cup shredded cheese, such as Monterey jack or Cheddar • 1 tbsp extra-virgin oil • 2 ¾ cup flour (whole wheat) • 1 cup crumbled bran cereal (do not use bran flakes with raisins) • 2 tablespoons powdered baking soda • ½ quarts (liter) water

1. Preheat the oven to 350°F (180°C). Prepare two baking trays.

2. Shred the carrots and cheese with a grater.

3. In a large mixing basin, combine the carrots, cheese, and oil. In a smaller mixing dish, combine the dry ingredients. Add the dry ingredients to the carrot mixture, then stir in the water.

4. Place 1 tbsp of dough on a baking tray with a spoon. Repeat until the batter is gone. If desired, flatten slightly or leave as little balls.

5. Bake for 25 minutes until golden brown.

14

Training Treats

Positive reinforcement training is both enjoyable and effective for you and your dogs. We train our dogs on a constant basis and give them tiny pea-size goodies for excellent behavior and following instructions. We alternate rewards and praise on a regular basis, as well as providing a jackpot of many treats at once to keep them guessing what to anticipate.

Finding a treat that is easy to break into little pieces is the key to making useful training treats. Most dogs respond better to strong-smelling meat-based training treats. It's recommended to make your training treats at home with ingredients you know and trust.

Beef Heart Treats

Heart of beef is a nutritious and inexpensive dinner or treat. It's actually muscle meat, not a regular organ, because only 10% of your dog's diet should come from organs.

Preparation time: 10 minutes

Cooking time: 10 minutes

Quantity: 40 treats

1 lb. (450g) beef heart • a couple of tablespoons of olive oil

1. Cut the beef heart into small cubes.

2. In a large skillet over medium-high heat, cook the cubes in olive oil for about 10 minutes. Make several batches if they do not fit in a single layer.

3. After 5 minutes, you can add some dog friendly spices if you want.

4. Remove the cooked cubes to a paper towel to drain for about 30 seconds.

Liver Treats

Preparation time: 20 minutes

Cooking time: 1 hour

Quantity: 45 treats

2 cups whole-wheat flour • 1 lb. (450g) raw organic beef liver or chicken liver, washed • 1 egg • ½ cup of liquid

1. Preheat the oven to 350°F (180°C) and prepare a baking tray.

2. Puree the liver in a blender or food processor.

3. In a mixing dish, combine the liver purée, flour, egg, and water. Stir everything together thoroughly. As a result, you'll end up with a thick dough. Pour the batter on the baking sheet, then spread it out evenly.

4. Bake for 30 minutes. Remove the cookies from the oven and cut them into 1" (2.5cm) squares. Return the squares to the oven for another 10 minutes.

5. Turn off the oven and rotate the treats one final time. Leave the treats in the oven until it cools down to dry them.

Emergency Hot Dogs Training Treats

If you're in a hurry and need some training treats, these aren't the most luxurious or elaborate, but they are simple and quick to prepare. Use organic hot dogs as much as possible. The finest hot dogs to utilize are all-beef or turkey sausages.

Preparation time: 5 minutes

Cooking time: 10 minutes

Quantity: 100 treats

10 all-beef hot dogs

1. Each hot dog should be sliced into ten pieces.

2. Place six layers of plain paper towels on top of the hot dog slices.

3. Microwave the hot dogs for 5 minutes on paper towels, or until you feel they're done. Microwave cooking times will vary and you may need to use a low setting.

4. Remove the grease from the hot dogs' tops and turn them; microwave for another 2–3 minutes. When some hot dogs' margins begin to brown, they're ready to serve.

South Pacific Hot Dogs

Pineapple is high in calcium and potassium, which is beneficial for your dog. These nuggets can be made using all-beef, turkey, or organic hot dogs.

Preparation time: 10 minutes

Cooking time: 20 minutes

Quantity: 100 treats

10 all-beef hot dogs • ½ peeled, cored, sliced, and drained pineapple

1. Preheat the oven to 350°F (180°C). Prepare a baking tray.

2. Each hot dog should be cut into ten pieces. Cut the pineapple into equal-sized pieces.

3. On a baking tray, arrange hot dog slices and pineapple slices and bake for 20 minutes.

Squares of Chicken Liver

Preparation time: 10 minutes

Cooking time: 2 hours

Quantity: 50 treats

1 lb. (450g) chicken • 3 eggs • 1 lb. (450g) washed chicken liver

1. Preheat the oven to 200°F (95°C). Prepare two baking trays.

2. Combine the chicken and eggs in a blender or food processor. Stir all of the chicken liver juices into the mixture. Process until smooth.

3. Pour the mixture onto the two baking trays, it should have a thickness of 1"(2.5cm).

4. Bake for 1 hour, cut each mixture into 1" squares and flip the treats to brown all sides. Bake for another hour in the oven.

5. Turn off the oven when the treats are golden brown, but leave the baking trays inside to cool and dry for several hours.

Bites of Anchovy

Preparation time: 10 minutes

Cooking time: 25 minutes

Quantity: 36 treats

1 can (2 oz./50g) anchovies in olive oil (do not drain) • 1 cup of water • 1 egg • ½ cup oats, rolled • ½ cup flour (whole wheat) • 4 teaspoons parsley, finely chopped (fresh or dry)

1. Preheat the oven to 350°F (180°C). Line a baking tray with parchment paper or grease it.

2. In a blender, purée the anchovies, water, and egg.

3. In a big mixing basin, combine the oats, flour, and parsley. Fully incorporate the anchovy paste.

4. Make little dough balls with a small scoop and place them on a baking tray.

5. Bake for 25 minutes until golden brown.

Cheese Training Treats

In dog treat recipes, I often see people use garlic powder or garlic salt, since garlic has a strong odor that makes these desirable as a training treat. Do not do this since garlic is poisonous for dogs no matter the dosage. A small amount will not have a big effect on most dogs, but you should still be careful to avoid this in all your recipes as it kills off the red blood cells of your dog.

Preparation time: 30 minutes

Cooking time: 15 minutes

Quantity: 25 treats

1 cup flour (whole wheat) • 1 cup Cheddar cheese, grated • 1 tbsp soy sauce • 1 tbsp softened butter • ½ gallon (1,9l) milk

1. Use your food dehumidifier or preheat the oven to 350°F (180°C). Line a baking tray with parchment paper or grease it.

2. Hand-mix all ingredients except the milk in a large mixing bowl. Mix in the milk a little at a time until all of the ingredients are incorporated.

3. Knead the dough on a floured surface and roll it out to a thickness of ¼ inches (6mm).

4. Cut dough with cookie shapes of your choice and set on baking tray. Bake for 15 minutes, or until golden brown.

5. Turn off the oven, crack the oven door a little, and let the goodies cool entirely in the oven to make them extremely crispy.

Simple Crispy Cheese

These simple cheese bites are a terrific training treat if your dog doesn't have any problems digesting lactose. And maybe you'll discover they're as addicting as potato chips for the trainer.

Preparation time: 5 minutes

Cooking time: 5 minutes

Quantity: 16 treats

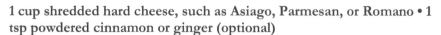

1 cup shredded hard cheese, such as Asiago, Parmesan, or Romano • 1 tsp powdered cinnamon or ginger (optional)

1. Preheat the oven to 350°F (180°C). Grease two baking trays.

2. Mix the spice powder with the cheese if using.

3. Simply layer or stack about 1 tbsp of cheese onto the baking trays. Allow some space between the treats because they will spread out. Even out the piles so that each one is about the same height.

4. Bake for 5 minutes.

Crouton Treats

Have you ever had stale bread that you didn't know what to do with? Croutons are easy to prepare and fun for you and your dog to eat. They also make excellent training treats due to their easy portability and crouton size.

Preparation time: 10 minutes

Cooking time: 40 minutes

Quantity: 60 small treats

6 large bread slices • ½ cup Parmesan cheese, grated • ½ cup bacon fat or olive oil, melted

1. Preheat the oven to 250°F (120°C).

2. Cut the bread into 1" (2.5cm) squares.

3. Combine the bread squares and Parmesan cheese in a large mixing dish. Pour olive oil or bacon fat over the bread, while mixing it.

4. Bake for 40 minutes, flipping halfway through to ensure uniform browning.

16

Dried Treats and Jerky

There are many questionable jerky products on the market, which means it's up to you to make your own jerky. There's no need to jeopardize your dog's health or your personal peace of mind because making your own nutritious jerky and chews for your dog is quite simple.

Homemade jerky chews also offer the benefit of allowing you to tailor the thickness and chewiness of the chew to your dog's preferences. You can create a softer chew for a senior or a tougher chew if you share your home with a young and active dog. Even better, you can create them all for a fraction of the cost of store-bought chews.

Strips of Dried Beef

Skirt steak is a great low-cost option. The hardness of this cut makes it a fantastic chew.

Preparation time: 15 minutes

Cooking time: 3 hours

Quantity: 60 treats

Skirt steak, 1 lb. (450g)

1. Use your food dehydrator or preheat the oven to 300°F (150°C). Prepare a baking tray.

2. Beef should be cut into ½-inch-wide strips (1.2 cm). Place the sheets on the baking tray, but make sure they aren't in contact.

3. After 1 hour of baking, reduce the oven temperature to 200°F (95°C). Open the oven door to allow moisture to escape. Bake the strips for another 2 hours.

4. Remove the strips from the oven and set them on a wire drying rack to cool.

Turkey Jerky Treats

Jerky for dogs is usually mild and unsalted, unlike human jerky. Teriyaki sauce can be replaced with low-sodium soy sauce or blackstrap molasses.

Preparation time: 20 minutes

Cooking time: 4 hours

Quantity: 120 treats

2 lb. (900g) lean turkey ground • 2 tbsp teriyaki sauce (optional)

1. Use your food dehydrator or preheat the oven to 200°F (95°C). Prepare a baking tray.

2. Turkey should be cut into ½-inch-wide strips (1.2 cm). Place the sheets on the baking tray, but make sure they aren't in contact.

3. After 2 hours of baking, turn the strips. Open the oven door slightly to allow moisture to escape. Bake the strips for another 2 hours.

4. Remove the strips from the oven and set them on a wire drying rack to cool.

Chicken Jerky

In recent years, there have been a number of issues with commercial chicken jerky chews, which has scared dog owners. Making your own easy-to-make chicken jerky ensures that your dog's meal is healthy and nutritious, without the use of preservatives or other additives.

Preparation time: 20 minutes

Cooking time: 4 hours

Quantity: 60 treats

1 lb. (450g) deboned chicken breasts

1. Use your food dehumidifier or preheat the oven to 200°F (95°C). Prepare a baking tray.

2. The chicken should be cut into ½-inch-wide strips (1.2 cm). Place the sheets on the baking tray, but make sure they aren't in contact.

3. After 2 hours of baking, turn the strips. Open the oven door slightly to allow moisture to escape. Bake the strips for another 2 hours.

4. Remove the strips from the oven and set them on a wire drying rack to cool.

Dehydrated Chicken Liver Treats

If you don't have a dehydrator, bake the chicken livers on the lowest temperature setting on a lightly greased baking tray for about 2 hours, turning halfway through.

Preparation time: 10 minutes

Cooking time: 4 hours

Quantity: 20-30 treats

1 lb. (450g) washed chicken liver

1. If some of the livers are excessively thick, flatten them slightly with a fork.

2. Place the livers on dehydrator trays, leaving enough space between them to allow for excellent air circulation.

3. Change the position of the drying trays when the livers are noticeably dryer, and let to dehydrate for another 4 hours. Drying times will vary depending on the dehydrator model.

Dehydrated Beet Chips

These chewy chips are a healthy alternative for dogs who like to chew on their snacks. Are you in a hurry? Buy sliced beets in a low-sodium can. Before baking, drain and rinse the beets.

Preparation time: 20 minutes
Cooking time: 40-50 minutes
Quantity: 25 chips

1 lb. (450g) beets, fresh • Olive oil

1. Preheat the oven to 350°F (180°C). Prepare a baking tray.

2. To get the most from your beets, it is critical that you clean and peel them. Remove the stems. Thinly slice.

3. Place the beet slices on parchment paper so that the edges do not touch. The slices can be lightly coated in olive oil.

4. Bake for 30–40 minutes. Turn off the oven and leave the beets in for another 10 minutes, then remove and cool on a wire rack.

Kale Chips

Green cabbage is ideal for canines in need of a low-calorie, high-nutrient treat. Dogs with kidney problems or bladder stones should it.

Preparation time: 30 minutes
Cooking time: 20 minutes
Quantity: 10-20 treats

1 head cleaned and dried kale • 2 tablespoons olive oil

1. Preheat the oven to 275°F (135°C). Prepare a baking tray.

2. Remove and discard the ribs from the kale, then cut it into 2-inch (5cm) pieces.

3. Mix the pieces with olive oil and place them on a baking tray.

4. Bake kale for 20 minutes, rotating leaves halfway through.

Dehydrated Sweet Potato Chews

These dehydrated sweets can be made in the oven if you don't have a food dehydrator. Sweet potatoes provide a nutritious and pleasant chew.

Preparation time: 20 minutes

Cooking time: 14 hours

Quantity: 10 chews per potato

sweet potatoes, medium

1. Remove any sprouts or green spots from the sweet potatoes before washing and peeling.

2. Cut the potatoes into ¼ -inch (0.6cm) slices. Slightly thicker slices will provide your dog more chewing pleasure but they will not dry up as quickly and have a shorter shelf life.

3. Arrange the slices on the trays to dehydrate. If the slices come into contact with one another, the edges will not dry properly.

4. For around 14 hours, dry the potatoes. If you want to use your oven, set the oven temperature to 200°F (95°C) and bake for about 6 hours.

17

Aspic, Broth, Gravy, Icing and Spices

For a long time, natural gelatin presents in cattle, veal, hog, poultry, and even some fish has been coaxed into producing aspic from thickened meat broth. It was an ingenious approach to keep the food from spoiling before modern. Although the usage of aspic and gelatin has diminished, you can expect that anything meat-derived will appeal to canine taste receptors.

The restorative power of soup and broth is something we have all experienced, whether it's Mom's homemade chicken soup when we're feeling sick, or as an appetizer before the main course of a meal. Dogs, too, love these tasty delights, and they are all easy to make and save for future use. This is also a good way to provide extra hydration to your pet.

Slow Beef Marrow Broth and Aspic

Making your own beef stock from marrow bones, jellied as aspic, can be very simple when using a slow cooker. The bones may be reused to produce additional batches of stock, but you'll need new ones for aspic.

Preparation time: 20 minutes

Cooking time: 34 hours

Quantity: 2-3 quarts (liter)

1 lb. (450g) beef marrow bones (beef feet recommended) • 2 tbsp. apple cider vinegar • 3 carrots, cut into 1-inch(2.5cm) rounds • 3 celery sticks, diced

1. Fill the slow cooker halfway with water and then add all of the ingredients on top of the bones. Set the temperature to low in the slow cooker.

2. Remove the bones after 8–10 hours. With a knife, push the marrow into the soup.

3. Cook for 24 hours on low.

4. Cool the soup before straining it and adding meat and veggies to your dog's food.

5. The minerals and marrow from the bones leak into the water and form the aspic when refrigerated. Refrigerate for up to 3 days or freeze for up to 6 months in an airtight container.

Basic Aspic

Aspic, a delicious gelatin made from vegetables and meats, is a centuries-old technique for cooking veggies and proteins. Aspic can be used in place of broth in dishes, as a low-calorie dessert, or as a complement to another dish.

Preparation time: 45 minutes

Cooking time: 6 hours

Quantity: 5 cups

2 lb. (900g) pigs' feet • water • 5–8 large drumsticks, thighs, or boneless chicken parts • 1 carrot, big • ribs of celery • 1 tsp salt

1. Soak the pigs' feet in cold water overnight and refrigerate.

2. Fill a large stockpot halfway with water and add the pigs' feet and the chicken. Bring the water to a boil. Remove the pot from the heat and pour away the water.

3. Fill with just enough cold water to cover the bottom of the pot. Bring to a boil, then simmer on low heat for 5 hours.

4. Add the carrots, celery, and salt to the pot. Simmer for 1 additional hour. Remove the meat and veggies from the pot. The pigs' feet and celery rib can be thrown away. Using a sieve, strain the broth.

5. Remove the chicken from the bones. Slice the carrots and place on the bottom of a medium bowl. Add shredded chicken on top. Slowly pour the broth over the chicken and carrots, then place the bowl in the refrigerator overnight.

6. The next day, put the bowl in hot water for a few seconds, then invert it onto a plate to release the aspic. If required, separate the aspic from the bowl with a slim spatula.

7. Refrigerate for up to 3 days, or portion out and freeze for up to 6 months in an airtight container.

Poultry Aspic

Making an aspic dish is a unique way to spice up Fido's meal. If you prepare the recipe in numerous tiny bowls the size of your dog's food, it also makes a charming display for special occasions.

Preparation time: 40 minutes

Cooking time: 4 hours

Quantity: 5-7 cups

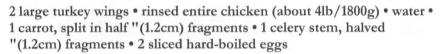

2 large turkey wings • rinsed entire chicken (about 4lb/1800g) • water • 1 carrot, split in half "(1.2cm) fragments • 1 celery stem, halved "(1.2cm) fragments • 2 sliced hard-boiled eggs

1. Remove the giblets from the chicken and save them for another use.

2. In a large stockpot, combine the chicken and turkey. Fill with just enough cold water to cover the bottom of the container. Bring to a boil over medium-high heat.

3. Skim the fat and froth away with a skimming motion. Add the veggies and return to a boil before simmering for 4 hours at low heat.

4. Remove the pan from the heat. Remove the chicken and turkey from the pan and shred the meat with two forks.

5. Remove the vegetables from the broth and save them for another recipe.

6. In the bottom of a large mixing bowl, place shredded meat. Add the egg pieces on top. Pour the strained broth over the mixture gently. Refrigerate for at least one night.

6. The next day, put the bowl in hot water for a few seconds, then invert it onto a plate to release the aspic.

7. Refrigerate for up to 3 days, or portion out and freeze for up to 6 months in an airtight container.

Stock of Beef

Many commercial stocks include onions, which you should never feed to your dog. Making your own dog-friendly Beef Stock is cheap and simple, and it will keep for quite some time.

Preparation time: 30 minutes

Cooking time: 4-6 hours

Quantity: 2-3 quarts (liters)

2 carrots, peeled and cut into cubes • 1 lb. (450g) stew meat (beef) • Marrow bones from 5 lb. (2250g) of meat • olive oil • 1 celery rib, peeled and cut into cubes • Water

1. Preheat the oven to 400°F (205°C).

2. In a big roasting pan, arrange the vegetables, stew meat, and bones. Coat the bones with olive oil. Roast for 45 minutes, or until meat and bones are browned, turning halfway through.

3. In a large stockpot, combine the bones, meat, and carrots, as well as the drippings and browned bits. Add the celery, then cover with cold water to 2" (5cm) above the bones.

4. Allow the stock to simmer on low heat for 4–6 hours. Let it cool down a bit and remove the bones.

5. Remove the vegetables and meat from the stock using a fine strainer. Use the vegetables and meat as a side dish or topping for your dog.

6. If you want to remove the fat, keep the liquid refrigerated. The fat will rise to the top of the liquid when it is cold.

7. It can be frozen in ice cube trays or in plastic zip-top bags. Beef stock is a delectable frozen treat that may be used many recipes.

Homemade Chicken Broth

Onion, a no-no for dogs, is found in conventional chicken broth, as well as too much sodium. Homemade Chicken Broth is fast and easy to make and can be used in many recipes.

Preparation time: 5 minutes

Cooking time: 60 minutes

Quantity: 2-3 quarts (liters)

1 chicken (3 lb. /1360g) • Water

1. Place chicken in a large stockpot and cover with 3" (7.5cm) of water. Bring to a boil, then simmer for 1 hour.

2. Remove chicken from the water and reserve for another recipe. Discard all cooked chicken bones because cooked bones are a choking hazard for dogs.

3. It can be frozen in ice cube trays or in plastic zip-top bags. Chicken broth is a delectable frozen treat that may be used many recipes.

Bacon Gravy

This gravy may be served with your dog's meal as a special-occasion topper. It is also a perfect way to disguise healthy ingredients in your dog's food.

Preparation time: 5 minutes

Cooking time: 15 minutes

Quantity: 1 ½ cups

6 bacon slices • 2 cups milk • 2 tsp all-purpose flour

1. In a large pan, fry the bacon over medium heat until crisp. Remove the bacon from the pan and break it into little pieces.

2. Remove the bacon fat from the pan and add two 2 tablespoons back to it.

3. Add the flour to the grease and stir continually. Pour in the milk and whisk constantly while the gravy thickens, lowering the heat after a minute. Stir in the bacon chunks. Simmer until desired thickness is reached.

4. Use up to one tbsp as a meal topping. Refrigerate for up to 3 days or freeze for up to 6 months in an airtight container.

Liver Gravy

To entice your dog to try new foods, spread a tablespoon of this delicious sauce over the dish you're attempting to introduce him to. You can use it to make frozen ice cubes for a delicious summer treat!

Preparation time: 10 minutes

Cooking time: 15 minutes

Quantity: 1 gallon (3.8l)

1 tbsp olive oil • 1 pound chicken liver, washed • 1 gallon (3.8l) chicken broth

1. Cook liver in oil in a large skillet over medium-high heat until golden.

2. Remove the liver from the heat and purée it in a blender. Pour in the chicken broth. Pulse until smooth.

3. Refrigerate for up to 3 days or freeze for up to 6 months in an airtight container.

Turkey Gravy

Whenever you roast a turkey, save the drippings for this dish. This quick turkey gravy is a fantastic addition to your Thanksgiving dinner, but it also makes a nice meal for your dog every day. To use as a meal topper, add up to 1 tablespoon per serving.

Preparation time: 20 minutes

Cooking time: 10 minutes

Quantity: 2 cups

2 cups drippings from the pan • ¼ cup all-purpose flour • 1 cup of water

1. The fat can be filtered out by chilling the drippings and removing the fat from the top. Use ¼ cup of fat for this recipe.

2. Heat the fat in a large skillet over medium-high heat, then add the flour.

3. Stir continually for about 1 minute. Reduce to desired thickness by adding turkey drippings, stirring constantly. If needed add some water.

Gravy with Giblets

This gravy is excellent for topping your dog's vegetables, rice, or any other dish. Simply add a spoonful to your dog's dinner for a delightful treat.

Preparation time: 30 minutes

Cooking time: 75 minutes

Quantity: 1.5 quarts (liters)

1 tbsp oil (vegetable) • 1 turkey's neck and giblets • 1 chopped celery rib 1 sliced carrot • four cups of water • 2 quarts (liters) chicken stock • 2–3 tablespoons flour (all-purpose)

1. Place the neck and gizzards in a large saucepan over medium heat. Brown the meat, then add the rest of the ingredients (excluding the flour).

2. Cook for about an hour. Remove the pan from the heat.

3. Using a fine sieve, strain the broth. Fat should be skimmed off.

4. Remove the meat from the bones and discard them. Meat should be diced finely. Reheat the meat in the broth with the flour, stirring constantly. Bring to a boil, continually stirring, until the gravy thickens.

Chicken Gravy

This easy sauce may be used in a variety of ways to enhance the taste of your dog's meals. It can be used as a delectable topper, a flavorful complement to a stuff able treat, or a simple way to add variety to your dog's diet. Use up to one tbsp as a meal topping.

Preparation time: 10 minutes

Cooking time: 10 minutes

Quantity: 1 cup

2 tbsp melted butter • 2 tbsp flour (all-purpose) • Homemade Chicken Broth (1 ¼ Cups) • ½ gallon (1.8l) milk

1. In a large skillet, melt the butter over medium heat. Whisk in the flour and cook for 1 minute in the butter, stirring constantly.

2. Add the broth and milk, mixing thoroughly for about 2 minutes to thicken. Remove the pan from the heat and set aside to cool.

Mashed Potato Icing

Make a delicious dog biscuit or cupcake even more unique by decorating it with this icing for a special occasion. This healthy icing can be used in place of traditional white sugar icing.

Preparation time: 15 minutes

Cooking time: 25 minutes

Quantity: 2 servings

10 potatoes of a medium size • 2 tbsp. fresh parsley, chopped • 2 quarts (2l) of water • 2 tbsp. sour cream

1. Wash and peel potatoes, removing any green areas. Place potatoes in a large saucepan, cubed. Cover with water and add the parsley.

2. Bring to a boil, then simmer for 25 minutes on low heat.

3. Remove the potatoes and parsley from the water and mash them with a fork or a potato masher.

4. Mix with the sour cream. Combine with a fork or a whisk to make a smooth, lump-free mixture.

5. Allow to cool completely before serving. Refrigerate for up to 5 days or freeze for up to 6 months in an airtight container.

Cream Cheese Icing

This icing is perfect for a healthy dog treat. It is made with cream cheese and yogurt, both of which are quite tasty for your pup.

Preparation time: 10 minutes

Quantity: 1 cup

8 oz. (225g) cream cheese • 2 tbsp plain low-fat yogurt • 2–3 tbsp flour (all-purpose)

1. In a mixing bowl, combine cream cheese and yogurt. Add the flour in a thin stream, mixing well after each addition until you reach the desired consistency.

2. After decorating, keep the frosting and treats refrigerated. Refrigerate for up to 5 days or freeze for up to 6 months in an airtight container.

Calcium from Eggshells

Calcium is very important for your dog 's health, especially when it comes to their bones and teeth. Eggshells are a great way to give them the calcium they need. Here's a way to create your own supplement from eggshells that would otherwise go to waste.

Preparation time: 30 minutes

Cooking time: 15 minutes

Quantity: 12

12 eggshells or more

1. Refrigerate washed eggshells until you have enough to cover a baking tray.

2. Preheat the oven to 200°F (95°C).

3. Bake the eggshells for 10–15 minutes after spreading them out on a baking tray. Before grinding, the eggshells must be completely dry.

4. With a mortar and pestle, grind to a fine powder. You can also use a clean coffee grinder or blender. If using a blender, make sure to grind the eggshells until all large pieces are ground to a powder.

Flavor Powder

You can turn this powder into a gravy or sprinkle it on your dog's food to add flavor. This recipe makes will keep for 1 month in the fridge or 6 months in the freezer.

Preparation time: 30 minutes

Quantity: 1 box of spices

1/2 cup dried beef or chicken • 1 cup freeze-dried liver • 1/2 cup low-salt beef bouillon powder (without onions) • 1/2 cup parsley flakes • 1/2 cup dried carrots • 1/2 cup celery flakes • 1/2 cup dried tomato flakes • 1/2 cup brewer's yeast (powdered) • 1 tablespoon red beet powder

1. Place the dried liver in a blender and process into a powder.

2. Put the dried meat into the blender and blend until the pieces are very small.

3. Add the remaining ingredients and blend until you're happy with the consistency.

Frozen Treats for Hot Days

Do you want to know how to keep your dog cool during the hot summer months? Frozen treats can be ideal for this task. Some dogs like the crunch of frozen treats, while others demand that the food is slightly warm

Frozen treats are also great for keeping your dog occupied. If you have a dog that loves to chew, frozen treats will keep them busy for a while.

Beef Popsicle Treats

During the summer, it's even more crucial to keep your dog hydrated. With this easy-to-make beef popsicle, your dog will enjoy a yummy, chilly treat.

Preparation time: 30 minutes

Cooking time: 45 minutes

Quantity: 35-40 treats

1b (450g) beef mince • 1 lb. (450g) peas (fresh, canned, or frozen) • 7 cups water (distributed)

1. Combine the ground beef, peas, and 2 cups water in a blender.

2. Mix on low until the mixture is smooth. Add 1 cup of water and increase the speed to purée it for 1–2 minutes.

3. Fill a large pot halfway with the ingredients. If you wish, any fat that has adhered to the blender may be removed.

4. Pour in the remaining 4 cups of water. Bring to a boil over high heat and simmer for 30 minutes at a steady boil. Remove the pan from the heat.

5. After the mixture has completely cooled, pour it into plastic tubs or ice cube trays. Freeze for at least 24 hours.

Bacon Ice Cream

Everything tastes better with bacon, even ice cream. Your pup will love this savory treat and you can use it as a reward after a training lesson, a vet visit, or a nail trim.

Preparation time: 10 minutes

Freezing time: 24 hours

Quantity: 22 ice cubes

1 cup plain low-fat yogurt • 3 cooked bacon pieces, finely crumbled • 1 tsp bacon grease

1. Combine all ingredients in a large mixing bowl.

2. Fill ice cube trays halfway with the mixture and freeze.

3. Freeze for up to 6 months in an airtight container.

Carrot Popsicle

These healthy treats are a great way to cool down your dog on a hot day. To use as training treats, aim to make them as tiny as possible.

Preparation time: 40 minutes
Cooking time: 25 minutes
Quantity: 36 treats

4 ounces cream cheese (low-fat) • 1 cup carrots, finely grated • ½ cup peanuts, unsalted

1. In a mixing dish, combine cream cheese and carrots.

2. In a blender or food processor, grind the peanuts to a fine powder. Pour out the powder on a clean surface.

3. Make small balls out of the cream cheese mixture, about 1" (2.5cm) in diameter. Roll them in peanut powder.

4. Place the balls on a plate or baking tray and freeze for 4 hours.

Chicken Broth Popsicles

On hot days, this simple frozen treat is a great way to encourage your dog to drink more!

Preparation time: 20 minutes
Cooking time: 8 hours
Quantity: 30 servings

½ quarts (liters) of water • 1 lb. (450g) of chicken meat

1. In a 4-quart/liter (or bigger) slow cooker, combine the water and chicken meat. Cook the chicken in the slow cooker on low for at least 8 hours. Remove the bones and skin from the mix if you're using whole chicken parts. Return the chicken to the slow cooker after shredding any large pieces.

2. The mixture should be stirred. Fill plastic cups or ice cube trays halfway with the broth mixture. Stir between each popsicle to ensure that each frozen treat contains chicken chunks.

3. Freeze for at least 24 hours.

Peanut Butter Ice Cream

Doggie ice cream is quite simple and inexpensive to make at home. This recipe only requires 3 ingredients, and your dog will love it!

Preparation time: 5 minutes
Quantity: 50 treats

3–4 bananas, ripe • 4 cups plain low-fat yogurt • ½ cup unsweetened organic peanut butter

1. Peel the bananas and puree with yogurt and peanut butter in a blender.

2. Pour into ice cube trays and freeze

3. Store for up to 6 months in an airtight container.

Pumpkin Ice Cream

This delightful frozen treat might persuade you to compete with your dog for it. It's simple to prepare, and it's healthy.

Preparation time: 5 minutes
Quantity: 36 ice cubes

1 cup pureed pumpkin • 1 cup plain low-fat yogurt • ½ cup unsweetened organic peanut butter

1. In a blender, combine the ingredients.

2. Pour into ice cube trays and freeze

3. Store for up to 6 months in an airtight container.

Watermelon Slush

Watermelon is a healthy, low-calorie way to cool off during the summer heat. Watermelon is high in potassium and magnesium, as well as vitamins A and C, and it's also high in fluid, which helps to prevent dehydration.

Preparation time: 10 minutes
Freezing time: 24 hours
Quantity: 56 ice cubes

2 cups seedless watermelon cubes • ½ cup hulled strawberries • 1 tbsp molasses • ½ cup cultured coconut water • 1 lb. (450g) of ice

1. In a blender, combine all of the ingredients and blend until smooth.

2. Pour into an ice-cube tray and freeze. You may also utilize this as a slushie treat rather than ice cubes.

Popsicles with Blueberries

This ice cream is made with fresh blueberries, making it a perfect way to use up summer's bounty. Blueberries are high in antioxidants and vitamin C.

Preparation time: 10 minutes
Quantity: 28 ice cubes

1 lb. (450g) of blueberries • 1 cup plain low-fat yogurt

1. In a blender, puree the blueberries and yogurt.

2. Fill an ice cube tray halfway with the mixture.

3. Freeze for at least 24 hours. Transfer frozen cubes to a zip-top plastic bag and keep in the freezer for up to 2 months.

Banana Ice Cubes

These banana ice cube treats are ideal for powerful dogs that need to burn off energy. Fresh and delectable!

Preparation time: 5 minutes

Quantity: 42 ice cubes

1 very ripe banana • water

1. Slice the banana in pieces and put them into an ice cube tray.

2. Fill with water. The overly ripe, mushy bananas will permeate the entire ice cube with their flavor.

3. Freeze for at least 24 hours. Transfer frozen cubes to a zip-top plastic bag and keep in the freezer for up to 2 months.

Caribbean Canine Coolers

This dish is ideal for bananas that have started to go soft. The sweet flavors of the dish will remind you of the islands, and your dog will love it!

Preparation time: 5 minutes

Quantity: 42 ice cubes

3 cups yogurt (plain) • 1 cup unsweetened crushed coconut flakes • 1 tbsp molasses (blackstrap) • 2 peeled huge mango • 2 peeled bananas

1. In a blender, combine all of the components and mix for 1–2 minutes until smooth.

2. Freeze this mixture in ice cube trays or tiny plastic tubs half-filled with it for a delicious island treat for you and your dog!

Frozen Fruit Popsicles

Blueberries and strawberries are favorite fruits among many dogs; some dogs like melons, peaches, and apples instead. This dish is simple to modify to your dog's favorite fruits. To make them sweeter and nourishing, molasses is added to these popsicles as some dogs are hesitant to consume fruits for the first time. Because the fruit has carbohydrates, you don't need to add any extra sugar. Simply leave out the molasses if you want to.

Preparation time: 10 minutes

Quantity: 56 cubes of ice

1 cup fresh fruit of choice, cored and diced (no grapes or raisins!) • 4 cups of water • 1 tbsp molasses (blackstrap) (optional)

1. Combine the fruit, water, and molasses (if using) in a large mixing basin.

2. Freeze the mixture in tiny tubs or ice cube trays. Store in a zip-top plastic bag in the freezer for up to 6 months once frozen.

Sorbet de Mango

Is your dog lactose intolerant? This delicious dairy-free dessert is a wonderful ice cream substitute for you and your dog! The mango, India's national fruit and a major part of Ayurvedic therapy, is high in vitamin C. While there are several varieties of mangos, they all have a nutritional punch. This fruit contains more than twenty vitamins and minerals in addition to being low in fat, sodium, and cholesterol.

Preparation time: 10 minutes

Quantity: 28 ice cubes

2 peeled ripe mangos • 1 orange's juice • ½ cup almond milk, unsweetened

1. Purée all of the ingredients in a blender.

2. Fill an ice cube tray halfway with the mixture.

3. Freeze for at least 24 hours. Transfer frozen cubes to a zip-top plastic bag and keep in the freezer for up to 2 months.

Raw Nuggets

These flavorful and nutritious nuggets are sure to wow as a training incentive or a healthy snack. Alfalfa sprouts are high in vitamins A and C, as well as chelated minerals, plant proteins, fiber, and other nutrients.

Preparation time: 10 minutes
Freezing time: 24 hours
Quantity: 50 treats

1 lb. (450g) lean ground turkey, lamb, or beef, uncooked • ¼ cup fresh parsley, chopped • ¼ cup alfalfa sprouts, chopped • ¼ cup sesame seeds

1. Combine the meat, parsley, and sprouts in a mixing dish.

2. Make small balls with a size of 1" (2.5cm) out of the mixture. Sprinkle sesame seeds on top. Continue until all of the ingredients have been utilized.

3. Place on a plate or baking tray and freeze for a few hours. Once the balls have been frozen, place them in airtight containers. They can be kept in the freezer for up to 6 months.

Raw Crunchy Treats

These frozen treats are a fast and simple raw snack. Make sure they're eaten as soon as possible after thawing.

Preparation time: 15 minutes
Quantity: 40 treats

1 lb. (450g) lean ground turkey, lamb, or beef, uncooked • ¼ cup molasses • 1 egg • ½ cup chopped pumpkin seeds

1. Combine the meat, egg, and molasses in a large mixing basin.

2. Pour down the chopped raw pumpkin seeds on a flat surface.

3. Form the meat mixture into 1" (2.5cm) balls by pinching off little pieces with your hands. Coat the balls in chopped pumpkin seeds.

4. Place on a plate or baking tray and freeze.

19

Imperial / Metric Conversion chart

In case you are unfamiliar with how to convert between Imperial and Metric measurements, this handy conversion chart should help.

U.S. Volume Measure	Metric Equivalent
$1/8$ teaspoon	0.5 milliliter
$1/4$ teaspoon	1 milliliter
$1/2$ teaspoon	2 milliliters
1 teaspoon	5 milliliters
$1/2$ tablespoon	7 milliliters
1 tbsp (3 teaspoons)	15 milliliters
2 tablespoons (1 fluid ounce)	30 milliliters
$1/4$ cup (4 tbsp)	60 milliliters
$1/3$ cup (5 tbsp)	90 milliliters
$1/2$ cup (8 tbsp / 4 fluid ounces)	125 milliliters
$2/3$ cup	160 milliliters
$3/4$ cup (6 fluid ounces)	180 milliliters
1 cup (16 tablespoons)	250 milliliters
1 pint (2 cups)	500 milliliters
1 quart (4 cups)	1 liter (about)

20

Conclusion

Thank you for reading my book! I hope you enjoyed it and found the information helpful. The journey you are about to take will be life transforming for you and your furry friend.

Please remember that this book can only act as a guide and you take responsibility for your dog's nutrition. The most important thing with homemade food is to make sure that you are mixing different types of food together so that your dog gets all the nutrients he or she needs. And remember to always change the ingredients, don't make the same meal over and over again! You can save some work by preparing a big batch of food that you then freeze in small portions. This way you will always have food ready for your dog.

Also, don't be afraid that this is too complicated or time consuming. You can easily make your own food; it becomes less time consuming after getting some practice. And always remember that you can use leftovers in your dogs' meal!

I really hope you enjoy this book and your dog enjoys the meals that you prepared.

I wish that you and your pet have a long, healthy life together.

Feel free to contact me if you have any questions or suggestions. You can reach me at:

EmmaRover@djts-publishing.com

Feel free to contact me if you have any questions or suggestions. You can reach me at:

EmmaRover@djts-publishing.com

We need your help:

It means a lot to us to get feedback from our readers. **Thank you very much** if you took the time to **leave a review on Amazon**!

pxlfy.me/xOcZ7q

Disclaimer / Imprint

Made in United States
Troutdale, OR
02/03/2024

17431117R00087